THE HYPOCRITE

THE HYPOCRITE is an historical play that drew its
initial inspiration from an incident in contemporary
Edinburgh and its relevance to modern morality does not
need emphasis. The Reverend Samuel Skinner, protagonist
of the play, is recognisable enough in present day Scot-
-land, but the life of this satirical comedy of manners comes
from the skill of Robert McLellan, probably the outstanding
Scottish dramatist of today in creating period, believable
characters and the authentic dialogue of the eighteenth
century. The reader will often be reminded of Sheridan
and Moliere, for the author creates not only the age, but
a style that is highly polished, witty and entertaining in
the classical manner.

Samuel Skinner, the protagonist, is a hypocrite of
impressive stature, his public puritanism and private
lechery going as naturally together as one would expect
from such an unpleasant person. The other characters
are all strongly drawn and memorable, each an
individual personality, throwing some light on the
colourful age they inhabit. The play was first performed
at The Royal Lyceum Theatre in Edinburgh, and was
successfully received by critics and public. The
publication in this series should help to make the work
of this much admired playwright available outside
Scotland and lead to wider performances.

Robert McLellan was born in 1907 at Kirkfieldbank on the
River Clyde and educated in Scotland. His many plays
have been widely performed in the North and THE FLOWERS
O EDINBURGH and YOUNG AUCHINLECK have been
performed at the Edinburgh Festival. His best-known
play JAMIE THE SAXT is now required reading at many
universities and is separately published by Calder &
Boyars Limited in 'The Scottish Library. '

PLAYSCRIPT 19

'the hypocrite'

robert mclellan

CALDER AND BOYARS · LONDON

First published in Great Britain 1970
by Calder and Boyars Limited
18 Brewer Street London W1

Printed in Great Britain by
The Pitman Press,
Bath, Somerset

To Kate with love

THE HYPOCRITE was first performed on 2 August 1967 at the Royal Lyceum Theatre, Edinburgh, with the following cast

TOWN CRIER	John Porter Davison
MRS LUCY LINDSAY	Clare Richards
LORD KILMARDINNY	Walter Carr
JENNY GILLIES	Judith Carey
REV. SAMUEL SKINNER	Leonard Maguire
SIMON ADAIR	John Shedden
SIGNOR GIORGIO BAROCCI	Tom Conti
PHEMIE, LADY KILGALLON	Marillyn Gray
JOSEPH SKINNER	Kenneth Poitevin
KITTY	Brigit Forsyth
REV. DAVID KEMP	Martin Heller
ROBIN DOW	Tony Kinnie
NEIL BELL	Richard Wilson
QUEENIE	Janet Michael
JOHN DRUMMOND	Hugh Evans
JAMES HAY	Brian Carey
MUNGO MEIKLE	Walter Carr
SAUNDERS WATSON	James Gibson

CARRIERS
Victor Vincent, Russel Laing, Frank Wright

TOWNSPEOPLE
William Forsyth, Stuart Forbes, Simon Scott

The play was directed by Richard Eyre

THE HYPOCRITE

CHARACTERS

TOWN CRIER
MRS LUCY LINDSAY, a grass widow
LORD KILMARDINNY, a judge, her uncle
JENNY GILLIES, her maid
THE REV. SAMUEL SKINNER, D.D., of the Tolbooth,
    Edinburgh
SIMON ADAIR, Master of Allander, a Writer to the Signet
SIGNOR GIORGIO BAROCCI, an Italian engraver ·
PHEMIE, Lady Kilgallon of Auchengool
JOSEPH SKINNER, son of the Rev. Samuel Skinner, a
    manufacturer
KITTY, wife of Joseph Skinner, and daughter of Lady
    Kilgallon
THE REV. DAVID KEMP of Auchengool
ROBIN DOW, elder in Auchengool
NEIL BELL, landlord near Perth of the Bridge End Tavern
QUEENIE, his daughter
JOHN DRUMMOND, Provost of Perth
JAMES HAY, a Perth baillie
MUNGO MEIKLE, a baron baillie to the Earl of Allander
SAUNDERS WATSON, elder in the Tolbooth, an undertaker

CHAIRMEN   CADDIES   FISHWIVES

The Action takes place in 1760

PROLOGUE

(The Saltmarket, Edinburgh.

A stylised representation of the Saltmarket, Edinburgh, as it was about the middle of the eighteenth century. This should be capable of being faded out to bring up each of the scenes involved in the action of the play. CADDIES may be used between scenes to change properties, as required.

The Prologue opens with a combination of ballet and parade of the characters of the play, those not subsequently involved in the action being CHAIRMEN, FISHWIVES, CADDIES and a TOWN CRIER.

Street cries, perhaps, from the FISHWIVES, blending with musical accompaniment. CADDIES may pass with SIGNOR BAROCCI's cases of paintings and engravings, followed by BAROCCI himself. CHAIRMEN may bring on MRS LUCY LINDSAY in a sedan chair, from which she may alight, enter a stair bottom and disappear. Others pass up or down on their various concerns.)

TOWN CRIER. An exhibition will be held in Yaxley Davidson's hoose at the Cougair Port, frae Monday first, atween the hours o ten i the forenune and five i the efternune, at the whilk Signor Barocci, the famous engraver, will display original warks o Italian art, by Raphael, Titian and Tintoretto, forbye engravings o his ain execution, efter the famous maisterpieces in the Sistine Chapel and the Farnese Palace, Rome, by Michelangelo, Raphael and ither sichlike famous men o genius. Price o admission, three shillings.

(He goes off ringing his bell.

Street cries and music.)

ACT ONE

(MRS LUCY LINDSAY's flat in the Lawnmarket,
Edinburgh. The parlour. Doors from the stair landing,
and from an inner room.

LORD KILMARDINNY is discovered sitting. MRS
LUCY LINDSAY enters to him from the inner room.)

LUCY. Uncle Tom.

KILMARDINNY. Lucy.

(She holds up her cheek for him to kiss)

LUCY. Will you have some tea?

KILMARDINNY. I daurna bide. I'm ower thrang. I hae
twa lang memorials to digest for a case comin up in
the mornin, and if I dinna win back to them sune I'll
be oot o my bed aa night. I hae heard from the Faculty
o Procurators.

LUCY. What do they say?

KILMARDINNY. They hae ruled that you're the deserter
nou.

LUCY. But, uncle, you know that's a lie. He left me and
ran away to London. He said to establish himself and
then send for me. But he didn't mean it. The faculty
know he didn't mean it. They wouldn't have given me
a pension if they had believed him.

KILMARDINNY. Ye gat yer pension because he didna

manage to establish himsell, and couldna afford to keep ye. The faculty made enquiries. But he's established himsell nou in Jamaica, he says, and he wants you to gang oot and jeyn him.

LUCY. He doesn't. He's just saying it, knowing I won't.

KILMARDINNY. Weill, Lucy, as lang as he says it, and you dinna pit him to the test, the faculty says it has a soond case for withdrawin yer pension.

LUCY. And are they going to?

KILMARDINNY. Ay. They'll let ye hae it for twa months mair, and assist yer passage to Jamaica, but efter twa months, gin ye haena sailed, they'll accept nae responsibility for ye.

LUCY. Well, it was only twelve pounds. If I scrape I can manage without it.

KILMARDINNY. Ay, but I dout yer father's faculty'll follow the procurators.

LUCY. The surgeons?

KILMARDINNY. I dout sae.

LUCY. But if I hadn't married I'd have had a pension for life, as my father's dependant.

KILMARDINNY. Ay, Lucy, but ye did mairry, and nou ye're yer husband's dependant.

LUCY. But he's left me.

KILMARDINNY. If the procurators rule that you're the deserter, nou that yer man's able and willin' to hae ye, the surgeons arena likely to disagree, when it's gaun to save them siller.

LUCY. But, uncle, with both pensions gone, what will I do?

KILMARDINNY. Ye could aye pit the scoundrel to the test.

LUCY. Go out there and join him? Never.

KILMARDINNY. Na. Weill, I sympathise. I aye wonert
what ye saw in him. He was handsome, I daursay, till
he began to debauch himsell. And he was clever, in a
way, though crookit. I canna say I'll blame ye gin ye
refuse to jeyn him.

LUCY. But how am I to live?

KILMARDINNY. Weill, Lucy, I daursay I could manage
to raise my ain allouance a wee.

LUCY. Oh, Uncle Tom, I wasn't hinting at that. Nothing
was further from my mind.

KILMARDINNY. I'm shair no, but unless ye tak the boat
to Jamaica, and pit yersell at that scoundrel's mercy
again, I dinna see what else we can dae about ye. And
I dae no sae badly on the bench, and though I'm
extravagant in things like books and claret I'm a
bachelor, wi naither wife nor family to support, sae
I aye a pickle to spare. Dinna fash aboot takin a bit
favour, my dear.

LUCY. Oh but, Uncle Tom, I'd feel such a drain on you.

KILMARDINNY. Deil the bit: though mind ye, that
scoundrel suld be keepin ye, no me. Gin it hadna been
for the scandal it wad hae caused ye could hae been
free o him. Ye had grunds for divorce ten times ower.
But he was the deserter then, and the twa faculties
were willin to help ye, and it haurdly seemed worth
while to mak the haill maitter public. Divorce is ugly.
It stirs up dirt.

LUCY. There was never any dirt in my life to stir up,
Uncle Tom.

KILMARDINNY. I'm shair no. But an unscrupulous
coonsel for the defence can mak glabber oot o guid
clean mouls. (Partly in fun) Thae tea pairties o

yours, for instance, wi play-actors frae the Teylers'
Haa, and penters frae St. Luke's Academy.

LUCY. Oh, Uncle Tom.

KILMARDINNY. I ken. I ken. I'm no sayin they arena aa
as innocent as Adam. Aa I'm sayin' is that ance ye win
into the divorce coort, there's nae sayin what's gaun
to be said aboot ye, and it's better no to risk it.

LUCY. It would have been the best thing from the beginning,
Uncle Tom.

KILMARDINNY. Na na. It wasna the best thing at the time,
and I dout if it wad be the best thing nou; though mind
ye, we could mebbe stop juist short o it. We could at
least hae him watchit.

LUCY. Out in Jamaica?

KILMARDINNY. Ay, Fairbairn and Witherspune are
stertin a brainch oot there, and they could arrange to
hae the job dune for me. I'm shair that if it was weill
watchit he wad be fund up to his auld tricks within a
week, though they say there's a dearth o weemen oot
there.

LUCY. (Rather eagerly) Then you wouldn't object to a
divorce for me after all, Uncle?

KILMARDINNY. I dout if we wad need to gang as faur as
that, gin we could win prufe o his infidelity. A word
to the Faculty o Procurators and they micht weill
cheynge their rulin aboot wha was the deserter.

LUCY. You think they would give me back my pension?

KILMARDINNY. Ay, and the surgeons micht tae. It's
worth tryin.

LUCY. (Persisting) But if you did get proof of infidelity,
and the procurators wouldn't alter their ruling, would
you agree to a divorce for me then?

14

KILMARDINNY. (Suspiciously) Lucy, my dear, what dae ye want a divorce for? There isna someone else in yer mind, is there? For I warn ye to be carefou. Ony scandal, my dear, and yer hopes o gettin back yer twa pensions are richt doun the stank. And though I dinna mind helpin ye, my dear, as the innocent pairty to a disastrous mairriage, I wad be laith to help ye to bide awa frae yer lawfou husband to hae a clandestine affair wi some blaggard wi nae mair scruple nor to mak advances to ye in yer praisent defenceless situation. Wha is it, Lucy? There is someane, is there? It isna ane o thae play-actors, is it? Or a penter?

LUCY. Oh, Uncle Tom.

KILMARDINNY. Oh, I dinna share the common opinion o them as a lot a useless riff-raff. I value their work. But there's nae dout they're freer in their weys nor ither folk.

LUCY. Uncle Tom, you are a silly. I like having unusual men around me. I admit it. Clever ones. (Quite unscrupulously) That's why I like you so much.

(He smiles complacently)

But I do make sure there's never the slightest ground for any scandal. You're the only one who's ever here alone. Except perhaps...

KILMARDINNY. Except wha?

LUCY. Except the minister.

KILMARDINNY. Oh, Skinner. Weill, his claith maks him a respectable eneuch visitor, my dear. But if we were to pey attention to aa we hear aboot him...

LUCY. Ah, yes, uncle, but they say it's money he's always after, so I'm as safe as a leper. In any case, I don't believe a word they say about him, for I'm sure he's as straight-laced as anybody in the Kirk.

KILMARDINNY. The straight-laced kind are gey aften the

15

warst, Lucy. Oh ay, it's the truith. Ye hear some unco
queer stories whan ye sit on the bench. But that reminds
me. Thae memorials. I maun hurry awa.

(Knock)

Oh.

(JENNY GILLIES opens the door from the landing,
and looks in)

JENNY. Dr.Skinner, mem.

LUCY. Oh. Show him in.

KILMARDINNY. I'll hae to gang.

LUCY. Oh, don't hurry away, Uncle Tom. You'll have
to stay and pass the time of day.

KILMARDINNY. I canna thole the man. I hear eneuch o
him in the kirk.

LUCY. Sssh. (As SKINNER enters) Good afternoon,
doctor. You know my uncle, Lord Kilmardinny.

KILMARDINNY. Efternune, doctor.

SKINNER. (Unctuous and sanctimonious in manner) Good
afternoon. Good afternoon. Yes, Mrs.Lindsay, we
have met before, in this very room. Still keeping a
close eye on her material interests, my lord?

KILMARDINNY. Weill, someane has to dae it, whan the
blaggard she mairrit winna.

SKINNER. Ah, yes, but I understand he is at last able,
as well as willing.

KILMARDINNY. That has still to be putten to the test,
doctor.

SKINNER. Oh, but surely? He's bluffing, do you think, to
avoid having to support her?

16

KILMARDINNY. Juist. He's coontin on the fact that she
  kens him ower weill to trust him, and winna risk gaun
  aa the wey oot there to Jamaica juist to fin that he
  canna maintain her efter aa.

SKINNER. But his circumstances can be investigated,
  surely?

KILMARDINNY. They will be. Dinna fash.

SKINNER. Good. Good. You see, Mrs. Lindsay, you're
  in excellent hands.

LUCY. Oh, I know. And Uncle Tom isn't only capable.
  He's generous. More than generous.

KILMARDINNY. Nou, Lucy, nane o that.

SKINNER. I can guess, my lord, and it does you credit.
  I only hope I can fulfil my own obligation to your niece
  with half your success.

KILMARDINNY. Your obligation?

SKINNER. As her minister. I have my duty in respect of
  her spiritual, as you of her material welfare, my lord.

KILMARDINNY. Weill, I'm shair ye'll fin yer responsibility a plaisent ane, doctor. Apairt frae a lamentable
  lack o judgment whaur men are concerned...

SKINNER. Ah yes, haha...

KILMARDINNY. ... she's no sic a bad craitur.

LUCY. Oh, Uncle Tom.

SKINNER. A charming young lady, my lord. An
  ornament to her family. And patient in adversity.
  Devoutly receptive to the will of God.

LUCY. Oh, doctor.

KILMARDINNY. Ay, weill. I leave her in your hands,

doctor. Impress on her the value o discretion.

SKINNER. Discretion?

KILMARDINNY. (Facetiously) Ay, in respect o her
gentlemen freinds. (Looking at SKINNER rather
impudently) She has some unco queer craiturs in here
for their tea. Try to knock some sense into her heid.
She's whiles a wee thing reckless o her reputation.

LUCY. Oh, Uncle Tom, you're not serious.

KILMARDINNY. Dae ye think no?

LUCY. Of course you're not. (Kissing him heartily)
Goodbye, Uncle Tom.

KILMARDINNY. Guid-bye, lassie. (Looking rather
smugly at SKINNER) Efternune, doctor.

SKINNER. (Coldly) Good afternoon, my lord.

(KILMARDINNY leaves)

LUCY. He was only joking, doctor.

SKINNER. Joking, yes. But how? At whose expense?
(Mimicking KILMARDINNY, rather nastily) 'She has
some unco queer craiturs in here for their tea.' I
have a feeling he was being personal. Offensive.

LUCY. Oh, doctor, no. He didn't mean that you were a
queer creature. He'd never be so rude. I'm sure the
thought never crossed his mind.

SKINNER. He was eyeing me with a kind of leer.

LUCY. No, doctor, you're quite wrong. He was poking
fun at me, not you, and quite good-naturedly. Just
before you came in he was warning me to be discreet
about the friends I entertained here, and suggesting
that perhaps some of my actor and artist friends
might cause gossip, but of course I told him that I
never on any account received any of these gentlemen

18

alone.

SKINNER. I see. That puts a different complexion on the matter. And if that was the kind of advice he was giving you, I heartily endorse it, though he's rather a peculiar person to be warning you against actors and artists. He's a patron of this new Edinburgh Company that's presenting plays in the Taylor's Hall.

LUCY. But there's no harm in that, surely?

SKINNER. You think not?

LUCY. The drama is one of the arts, doctor. It has attracted some of the greatest geniuses of the age. Shakespeare, for instance. You wouldn't say there was any harm in Shakespeare, surely?

SKINNER. No, Mrs. Lindsay, don't prevaricate. Why instance Shakespeare? Has there been the slightest suggestion of any intention to produce Shakespeare? Are we not just as likely to be offered the work of filthy fellows like Wycherley and Farquhar?

LUCY. Oh, come, doctor. What makes you say that?

SKINNER. (Severely) You see, my dear, you know what I mean. (Accusingly) You're obviously familiar with their work.

LUCY. Well, I know the sort of play they write. You have to make allowance for their period.

SKINNER. Come, Mrs. Lindsay. You aren't being straight with me. You've read them.

LUCY. Well, yes, but why not?

SKINNER. I knew it. I'm afraid your uncle doesn't set you a very good example, my dear.

LUCY. But my uncle didn't recommend them to me.

SKINNER. Perhaps not. But he's a subscriber to Allan

Ramsay's library, and if it wasn't for that library neither Wycherley nor Farquhar would have been heard of here. No no, my dear, your uncle may be very shrewd in his management of your material affairs, but he's a regrettable influence on your immortal soul.

LUCY. Oh, come, doctor. Just because he's a patron of the arts.

SKINNER. Yes, it sounds very well. But what does it mean? It means encouraging plays that teach people to think of adultery as no more than an amusing habit. Not only by subscribing to a library that stocks them in book form, but by helping to set up a company of loose-living people in the town here, to act them out before people's very eyes. Inviting people to watch their filthy goings-on in public. Imagine a father and mother sitting together, perhaps with a daughter, at a play where the hero, the hero I say, is planning with a friend how to trap a married woman into visiting him alone, for an immoral purpose. That sort of thing will destroy all our moral standards. It's sinful. It's wicked. It's an affront to decency. It ought to be prohibited by law. And your uncle encourages it. A judge, yet he's allowed himself to be enrolled as a patron. I suppose he thinks his support of value, yet I wonder anyone can take him seriously, considering the ridiculous views he sometimes expresses in those essays of his in the Idler.

LUCY. I think his essays are well written and very intelligent.

SKINNER. Oh, come come. How can you take a man seriously who writes an essay contending that Scotch authors can never excel in English, because it is not their natural tongue, and yet writes that very essay in English?

LUCY. The Idler sells south of the Border. I supposed he is entitled to write in a tongue he doesn't speak, for the benefit of those who speak it, even if he feels he can never excel in it.

SKINNER. Why don't you speak the same coarse broad
    Scotch as he does, if you admire his views so much?

LUCY. I'm not of my uncle's generation, and I speak as
    I was taught at school. In any case, we weren't
    discussing his speech, but his encouragement of the
    drama. You were suggesting that the new company
    would put on nothing but the plays of Wycherley and
    Farquhar. So far they've given us only recent
    London successes.

SKINNER. London, yes. A sink of iniquity.

LUCY. Even in London, doctor, standards are very
    different now from what they were at the Restoration.
    And the laxity then was a reaction against the puritan-
    ism of the Commonwealth.

SKINNER. I can hear your uncle and his kind in every
    word you speak. Mrs. Lindsay, my dear young lady,
    don't despise puritanism. It's a better guarantee of
    respect for female chastity than the laxity of the
    Restoration libertine. All this talk of encouraging the
    arts. It's very fashionable just now, and no doubt
    you want to feel that you're a little ahead of the times.
    It's natural in a lively young woman. But it has its
    dangers, and while I'm glad that your uncle has warned
    you against too great familiarity with these actors and
    artists you feel so interested in, I'm afraid he doesn't
    set you the sort of example likely to impress you that
    his advice is meant with any great seriousness.

LUCY. I'm sure my uncle has never been guilty of anything
    in the least dubious. He can't afford the slightest
    deviation from the strictest principle. He's a judge.

SKINNER. Just what I say. He can't afford it, yet he takes
    the risk. His encouragement of these filthy books.
    This company of actors. And actresses. Actresses!
    I ask you, Mrs. Lindsay. What woman could live that
    sort of life and remain respectable?

LUCY. Oh, but surely...

SKINNER. I know what I'm talking about. I hear all the scandal. And it doesn't stop at books and acting.

LUCY. What doesn't?

SKINNER. Your uncle's folly, my dear. He's a patron of the Musical Society.

LUCY. Doctor! What harm can there possibly be in music?

SKINNER. Not in music. But in the way it's presented. That festival in St. Cecilia's Hall. That oratorio.

LUCY. That was sacred music. The Messiah.

SKINNER. It should have been sacred. But what did they do with it? Used it as an excuse to dress up young girls as angels.

LUCY. They looked very pretty.

SKINNER. Mrs. Lindsay, they were half naked.

LUCY. Oh come, doctor. Bare arms.

SKINNER. More than their arms.

LUCY. Oh doctor. I often wear a gown showing just as much.

SKINNER. At a rout. At a ball. But not in a sacred oratorio. And I'm not sure that dancing itself isn't just another opportunity for provocation.

LUCY. Really, doctor. You don't suggest that when I dress for a ball I deliberately set out to be provocative?

SKINNER. I'm afraid I think it's a weakness of most attractive women, my dear, that they enjoy exercising their power over men, and fashionable balls give them licence to go further than modesty ought to approve.

LUCY. Do you really think so?

SKINNER. I do. But I don't wonder that even the most respectable of women think nothing of a low gown, my dear, when men like your uncle seem to condone much worse.

LUCY. Much worse?

SKINNER. Don't you know what I mean? The new St. Luke's Academy. He subscribed to that too.

LUCY. But surely, doctor, it was badly needed. You wouldn't have the country without a single school for artists. So few of them can afford to go to Rome.

SKINNER. That at least is a blessing.

LUCY. Then if St. Luke's is saving them from having to go to Rome, why are you against it?

SKINNER. It doesn't so much save them from having to go to Rome, as bring Rome here to Scotland.

LUCY. You mean religious ideas?

SKINNER. That, and worse. Drawing from the naked figure. Can you deny that they have a girl there who stands without a stitch of clothing on, in front of students, so that they can draw her?

LUCY. But that's always been the case, in teaching studios.

SKINNER. It's never been the case here in Scotland.

LUCY. Because there's been no teaching.

SKINNER. It's completely unnecessary. Surely men can learn to draw the clothed female figure without submitting a poor starving girl to the shame and humiliation of standing in front of them naked.

LUCY. No, doctor. What the clothes figure looks depends not only on the clothes, but on what's underneath them. And even what's underneath that. The students at St. Luke's study anatomy. The muscles. And even the skeleton. They have to, to be able to draw the clothed figure with real skill.

SKINNER. You are familiar with these men?

LUCY. The students? Some of them yes.

SKINNER. My dear Mrs. Lindsay, I sincerely do think you keep dangerous company. Consider the appalling implications of what you have just said. It is the man who cannot look at a woman without thinking of what is underneath her clothes who sees her most truthfully? Is it not more important that he should see into her mind? Into her soul?

LUCY. But we're talking of artists, doctor.

SKINNER. Exactly. Shouldn't the artist try to show the reality of the spirit, rather than that of the flesh?

LUCY. He has to show the one through the other, the spirit through the flesh.

SKINNER. You think he cannot suggest a woman's personality without revealing what is underneath her clothes?

LUCY. You're trying to make what I say sound foolish, doctor, but you can't really pretend that any man can look at a woman and think there is nothing underneath her clothes.

SKINNER. Surely we needn't consider whether there is anything underneath her clothes or not.

LUCY. Oh doctor. You can't just not consider whether or not there's anything underneath a woman's clothes, or a man's either. You know there's something. You may not try to imagine what it's like, but you must know it's there, and that it affects what you see.

SKINNER. Really, Mrs. Lindsay, this is becoming most indelicate.

24

LUCY. Is it my fault? You force me to say these things or lose the argument.

SKINNER. The argument is that any man who cannot look at a woman without thinking of what is underneath her clothes is no gentleman. And no woman ought to be compelled to earn her living by standing naked in front of men. We're talking of artists, Mrs. Lindsay, and St. Luke's Academy.

LUCY. Nobody is compelled to be a model, doctor.

SKINNER. I can't think of any girl doing it who wasn't compelled by indigence, unless she's an absolute strumpet. It isn't decent. If you had a daughter, Mrs. Lindsay, would you allow her to do such a thing? And if not, can an institution which offers such employment, and depends on it, be good; be admirable!

LUCY. I see nothing wrong with the employment of a model.

SKINNER. You haven't answered my question. Would you allow your daughter to do it?

LUCY. I have no daughter.

SKINNER. I said, if you had one.

LUCY. It can't be wrong to pose in the genuine interest of art.

SKINNER. You compel me to be blunt, Mrs. Lindsay. If you don't think it wrong, would you do it yourself?

LUCY. The necessity isn't likely to arise.

SKINNER. But if it did?

LUCY. I can't see any likelihood of it.

SKINNER. You're avoiding my question. You would be willing to do it, if a model was otherwise unobtainable?

LUCY. I wouldn't think it wrong, but...

SKINNER. But what?

LUCY. Well, I know some of the students. I meet them socially. The situation in my case wouldn't be the same as with a girl whose contact with them was purely professional.

SKINNER. You see, my dear, you can't give me a straight answer.

LUCY. Because your question isn't fair. The fact that you ask it involves you in thinking of me as a model, and your attitude to models isn't an artist's. You think they're indecent. I don't like to be thought of like that. That's why my answer was hesitant.

SKINNER. Aren't you simply admitting that if you acted as a model you would be indecent?

LUCY. No, I'm saying that if you think of me as a model you think of me as something indecent. The indecency is in your view of the matter.

SKINNER. Oh, come, Mrs. Lindsay. Any woman who appears undressed in front of men is indecent, surely?

LUCY. I don't think so, if the men are artists. (Suddenly struck by the thought) Or husbands! You've been married twice, doctor. (Beginning to enjoy shocking him) Did your wives never undress in your presence?

SKINNER. (Emphatically, but not very convincingly) Never! Never!

LUCY. Oh come. You've had children.

SKINNER. Mrs. Lindsay, this conversation is becoming exceedingly embarrassing.

LUCY. Who started it, doctor? It was you who introduced the subject of the model at St. Luke's Academy.

SKINNER. I had no idea you would defend the creature.

LUCY. You knew my uncle was a subscriber. You knew
he was my guardian and that he helps to support me,
and that I owe him my gratitude. Besides, I have
friends at the Academy. Men whom I respect. Men of
great talent. I felt compelled to defend them.

SKINNER. However well-meaning they may seem to be,
they are indulging in dangerous enthusiasms. I think
they threaten our moral standards. An artist may be
able to think of a naked girl as a mere object to be
accurately reproduced on a piece of paper or canvas,
but ordinary men are made of flesh and blood, and
have instincts and appetites, not wrong in themselves
but difficult to control in the face of needless
stimulation.

LUCY. Only artists attend St. Luke's Academy, doctor, so
how can these ordinary men you speak of be upset by
anything that goes on there?

SKINNER. They learn what goes on.

LUCY. But they don't see it.

SKINNER. They may think of it. They may imagine it.

LUCY. (Naughtily) You think that if they imagine it they
will have sinful desires?

SKINNER. You think to mock me, but it is true.

LUCY. Oh come.

SKINNER. It is true.

LUCY. Doctor? Do you imagine what goes on? Do you
have sinful desires?

SKINNER. (Pretending cunningly to be trapped by her
coquetry) All men have sinful desires, Mrs. Lindsay.
But some of us pray to God to be given strength to
resist them. The laxity I have been speaking of makes

it more difficult for us.

LUCY. Poor Dr. Skinner. Do you really find it difficult
to control yourself, when you think of things you
shouldn't?

SKINNER. Don't mock me, Mrs. Lindsay.

LUCY. When you think of the model at St. Luke's
Academy?

SKINNER. In spite of my cloth, I am like other men.

LUCY. When you see girls dressed as angels, at musical
festivals?

SKINNER. Please.

LUCY. When you see ladies groomed for a ball, showing
too much shoulder? (She shows a little shoulder)
Have I myself given you difficulty, doctor?

SKINNER. (Pretending fear) You are trying to provoke me.

LUCY. Showing my ankles, perhaps? (She shows her
ankles) I remember now sometimes thinking that you
did seem to notice them.

SKINNER. Mrs. Lindsay, I warn you, for both our sakes,
do not play with me. I try, God knows, to keep my
instincts under control, but I have been married, as
you have just said, and now I am alone, and I am not
old, and I find it hard sometimes to be content with
my lot. And when you provoke me like this, I warn
you, I find it hard to keep my head.

LUCY. (Half afraid) Really, doctor.

SKINNER. (In for the kill) You see, Lucy, I love you.

LUCY. You what!

SKINNER. I love you. I do. And if you were free to marry
me I would declare my love and ask you to be mine,

28

but because you are tied to this man and cannot free yourself I have to conceal my feelings, difficult as it is; and now I have failed. May God forgive me, but when you started to mock me, and tantalise me with your shoulders and your ankles, you looked so adorable that I couldn't contain myself. Lucy, please don't despise me. Pity me. Say you are not offended. Say you are not angry.

(Knock)

LUCY. Ssh! (Calling) Yes?

JENNY. (Opening door from landing) It's the Maister o Allander, mem, wi a foreign gentleman.

LUCY. Show them in. (Quickly, to SKINNER) I daren't turn them away. It would arouse suspicions. We can discuss our feelings some other time. Ssh!

(As SIMON ADAIR and BAROCCI enter)

Ah, Simon, how pleasant to see you. And this is Signor Barocci?

SIMON. It is indeed. Barocci, meet my dear friend, Mrs. Lindsay.

LUCY. Welcome to Scotland, Signor. Simon has told me so much about you that I think of you almost as an old friend.

SIGNOR. Ah, Mrs. Lindsay, of you also Simon has told me very much, and that I will meet the best friends of the arts in all Scotland in your at home, and that your uncle who is a lord will be my friend, and his friends also will attend, when I come to show my pictures to the Scotch.

SIMON. Don't misunderstand him, Lucy. He knows not to expect company here today. I brought him at once because you insisted that I should.

LUCY. But you are quite right. You know Dr. Skinner?

SIMON. I know of him, of course.

LUCY. Doctor, this is the Master of Allander, Simon
Adair. I'm afraid he's Episcopalian.

SIMON. Traditional in our family, doctor.

SKINNER. (Coldly) So I understand.

LUCI. Signor Barocci, this is a well-known Edinburgh
divine.

SIGNOR. Divine?

LUCY. Minister. Clergyman.

SIGNOR. Ah. A priest of your church?

LUCY. Well, yes, in a way. The minister of the Tolbooth
Church here. Dr. Skinner.

SIGNOR. Doctor?

LUCY. Of Divinity.

SIGNOR. Ah, divinity.

SIMON. Presbyterian, you know. I have explained.

SIGNOR. (His face falling) Ah, yes. I understand.
(Formally) How do you do?

SKINNER. (Coldly) I am very well, thank you.

SIMON. Signor Barocci has come to exhibit engravings of
some of the masterpieces of Italian Art in the main
towns of Scotland. It was my idea. I met him during
my Grand Tour, and thought his engravings from the
masters so true to the originals that an exhibition of
them here would enable many, who are too busy or
too poor to travel, to learn something of a body or
work hitherto out of their reach.

SKINNER. The, er, Signor's exhibition has been announced

by the Town Crier.

SIMON. That is so.

SKINNER. What is his, eh, what is your religion,
Signor...?

LUCY. Barocci.

SIGNOR. Religion? I am a Christian.

SIMON. (To BAROCCI) He means, what is your church?
(To SKINNER) Being Italian, doctor, he is naturally
of the Church of Rome.

SIGNOR. Si, yes. The Church of Rome.

LUCY. (Sensing trouble) Now, gentlemen, we mustn't
upset Signor Barocci as soon as he arrives in Scotland
by bringing up the subject of religion. It causes too
much bad feeling.

SKINNER. Nevertheless, the question of religion may have
to be considered, if he intends to exhibit works of so-
called religious art, and I gather from the announce-
ment of his exhibition that among the works he intends
to display are engravings of the ceiling in the Sistine
Chapel. The Sistine Chapel is in the Vatican, the seat
of the Pope.

SIGNOR. The ceiling is by Michelangelo, a great master.
Surely it is not to be condemned because he was not a,
what is it you say, eh, a...

SIMON. Presbyterian. (To SKINNER) Signor Barocci is
right. Great art cannot be dismissed because it adorns
a church other than our own.

SKINNER. Can it be great art if it pretends to represent
God, and invites the ignorant to worship an attempted
likeness in place of a reality?

SIMON. I don't think the Roman Church offers these
likenesses of Christ as something to be worshipped in

31

place of Him. What do you say, Barocci?

SIGNOR. No no. The statues and paintings of Christ and His Mother are to help our people to conceive what the Holy Family was like, but they are offered as statues and paintings, not as the holy presences themselves.

SKINNER. Signor...?

SIMON. Barocci.

SKINNER. Ay. I have been told by people I trust implicitly that your people kneel before these statues and paintings and pray to them.

SIGNOR. Excuse me, no. They pray to the holy presences of which the statues and paintings are a representation; a representation greater than the ungifted among our people could conceive for themselves.

SKINNER. Sir, you quibble.

SIMON. Come, doctor. Signor Barocci is a guest in our country.

SKINNER. A guest in our country cannot expect hospitable treatment unless he respects our institutions. The established church in this country is the Church of Scotland, Signor, and in our Church to attempt to represent God or Christ in a so-called work of art is considered sacrilege, and to bow down before such a representation is idolatry. Our authority is the Ten Commandments.

SIMON. You are refusing to accept Signor Barocci's assurance that his people do not worship their paintings and statues, but the presences beyond them.

SKINNER. That, Master, as I have already said, is a quibble.

LUCY. Please, doctor.

SKINNER. My dear Mrs. Lindsay, I dislike being unfriendly to a foreign visitor, but if he has come to encourage the people of Scotland to gape at works of sacrilege, forbidden by God Himself, for God spake these words, saying, 'Thou shalt not make unto thee any graven image, or likeness of any thing that is in heaven above, or that is in the earth beneath, or that is in the water under the earth. Thou shalt not bow thyself down to them, nor serve them.' These are God's own words, so if Signor Barocci has come to display such likenesses I can only warn him that I will do all in my power to rouse my Church, ay, and the civil magistrates of any town he visits, into taking any steps which may be necessary to ensure that he is prevented. My dear Mrs. Lindsay, I have to go. I hope I may see you again very soon. (Contemptuously) Gentlemen, I leave you.

(He walks to the landing door, opens it and leaves)

LUCY. Oh dear.

SIGNOR. Is it possible? Can he prevent me?

SIMON. He might make things difficult. If he succeeds in persuading the ministers to preach against your exhibition anyone who attends may find himself being disciplined by his kirk session. And if he can persuade the magistrates that your exhibition is an encourage-ment of Popery, which is outlawed here, they may forbid it.

SIGNOR. But what of your friends? Of your father, the earl? Of the lady here, her uncle, the lord? And all their friends? Are they not patrons of the arts? And will they not see that I have justice? I have come a long way. I have spent much money. Master, I trusted you.

SIMON. I had almost forgotten that people like Skinner existed. And they have such power to work up the mob.

SIGNOR. You think there is no hope?

LUCY. Oh surely, Simon. The doctor won't be able to do

more than frighten off the members of the High Flyer congregations, and I doubt if any of these would have attended the exhibition anyway. The Moderate side of the Church will be more broadminded than to listen to him.

SIMON. You may well be right.

LUCY. And in any case, he may just have been in a rather nasty mood. I'm not sure that he was pleased to have his visit here interrupted by yours. You know what he's like.

SIMON. Oh yes. He's said to be a great lady's man. Is he paying you particular attention?

LUCY. If he was, Simon, I would be too discreet to divulge anything.

SIMON. You would be keeping no secret. He is widely believed to be assiduous in his duties towards the lonely of his parish, particularly the unattached ladies. He is known as the Widows' Friend.

LUCY. I've heard, though, that to qualify for really serious attention they must have money. His late wives were both of them heiresses.

SIMON. Yes, but I'm sure he's not above enjoying the company of those without it, provided they are as attractive as you.

LUCY. My dear Simon, you are the most bare-faced flatterer I've ever met.

SIMON. Not at all, I assure you.

LUCY. You really think I'm attractive enough to be able to take his mind off the persecution of poor Signor Barocci?

SIGNOR. What do you say? Oh Simon, my friend, I do not wish that Mrs. Lindsay should sacrifice herself to such a man for my sake.

LUCY. Shall we say, Signor, that I shall sacrifice myself for the sake of art?

SIGNOR. Oh no, I beg. No sacrifice.

SIMON. She is joking, Giorgio. She means only that she will take advantage of his interest in her charming person to try to persuade him to be more tolerant.

LUCY. Exactly. I think I may have just enough power over him to force him to listen to me.

SIMON. In any case, he hardly has time now to stop the exhibition in Edinburgh. It moves at the end of the week.

LUCY. And where do you take it then, Signor?

SIGNOR. To Perth, is it?

LUCY. Oh, what a pity.

SIMON. Why?

LUCY. His influence is strong there. His son is married to the daughter of Sir Colin Kilgallon of Auchengool.

SIMON. What of it? My father's estate is much larger, and as close to the town as Sir Colin's.

LUCY. But the doctor was once the Minister of Auchengool, and on several occasions Moderator of the Perth presbytery. He will have influence with every minister in the county, except, of course, your father's nominee at Allander.

SIMON. There are surely other Moderates in the county.

LUCY. I know of none.

SIMON. I shall have to make immediate enquiries. Barocci, we must leave at once. When are you likely to see the doctor again, Lucy?

LUCY. He normally visits me once a week.

SIMON. What bad luck. The exhibition will be almost due in Perth hefore you can influence him.

LUCY. (With a knowing look) He may come sooner this time.

SIMON. Lucy, I hope you haven't been encouraging him to hope for favour from you?

LUCY. If he did, Simon, he would be quite at my mercy.

SIMON. I'm serious. Please, Lucy, don't trifle with him. I'm sure he could be vindictive.

LUCY. Don't worry. I'll be very careful.

SIMON. I do hope so. Well, Barocci, we must ask Mrs. Lindsay to excuse us.

SIGNOR. Yes, excuse, please.

LUCY. Don't look so worried, Signor. I'm sure you'll be able to hold your exhibitions. If the doctor does try to oppose them, they will be the better made known.

SIMON. A very good point. Yes, cheer up, Barocci. I'm sure everything is going to be perfectly all right. Goodbye, Lucy.

LUCY. Goodbye, Simon. Goodbye, Signor. I'm sorry you can't stay for tea.

SIGNOR. It would have been a great pleasure. But we are so worried by your friend, the doctor.

LUCY. He may prove to have been a blessing in disguise.

SIGNOR. Disguise?

SIMON. A figure of speech, Giorgio. Come.

(He opens the landing door for GIORGIO, and LUCY

follows them out.)

ACT TWO

(The library of Auchengool House. One door. Window looking out over rural landscape.

LADY KILGALLON sitting at bureau, working on household accounts. Enter to her, DR. SKINNER. She does not hear him.)

SKINNER. (Coughing) Hhm. Lady Kilgallon.

(She turns to him)

LADY K. Oh gude efternune, Doctor. I had nae idea ye were here yet.

SKINNER. I sent a message ahead with my baggage.

LADY K. I ken, but I didna hear ye come forrit, or see ye aither, though the winnock here looks straucht down the drive.

SKINNER. I thought you would realise that I would be strolling over from the manse. I wanted a quick word with Kemp and his session clerk, but he was out visiting.

LADY K. Is it kirk business that's broocht yet, then?

SKINNER. Yes. I want Kemp to use his influence with the Perth presbytery to prevent an Italian adventurer from holding an exhibition in the town of filthy Popish pictures. He tried to in Edinburgh at Yaxley Davidson's but I had him stopped. Davidson was summoned before his kirk session and threatened with public denunciation and loss of communion. He didn't argue.

LADY K. And ye say this Italian's for bringin his picturs here?

SKINNER. To Perth, yes. I've no idea where he intends to hold the exhibition, but I've no doubt we'll be able to find out in time to stop him.

LADY K. Ye say his picturs are filthy? Papish?

SKINNER. The whole thing's a scandal. He's been brought here by young Simon Adair, who met him in Rome when he was on his Grand Tour. The man's a Papist, and the pictures are sacrilegious, idolatrous and filthy.

LADY K. Filthy? Shairly no. The young Maister o Allander was aye a respectable eneuch laddie.

SKINNER. Episcopalian, remember. His father still keeps the old curate on at the castle as a private chaplain.

LADY K. Ay, but baith he and the son are dacent eneuch folk. Filthy, ye say? Hou filthy?

SKINNER. My dear Lady Kilgallon, I hesitate to tell you.

LADY K. Come, Doctor. Ye needna be bashfou wi me.

SKINNER. It would be a shock to your modesty.

LADY K. Hoot, Doctor, I dout I hae little o that left. Ever sin Sir Colin had his last stroke he's needit nursin like a bairn.

SKINNER. He's no better, then?

LADY K. He's waur, I dout. I canna see what pleisure life can be to him. I declare he wad be better awa.

SKINNER. Oh, Lady Kilgallon!

LADY K. Wait till ye see him for yersell. Helpless. Canna feed himsell. Canna wash himsell. Canna blow

his ain nose. Sae dinna talk to me aboot modesty,
Doctor. Forbye, ye're my dochter's guid-faither, sae
the talk's in the faimily. Filthy, did ye say the picturs
were?

SKINNER. There's no other word. They're just not fit to
be seen by Christian people.

LADY K. I see. Nakit weemen?

SKINNER. Yes, and naked men.

LADY K. Na!

SKINNER. Yes, I assure you, my dear Lady Kilgallon.
Dozens of naked men. I might almost say hundreds,
in every conceivable sort of attitude.

LADY K. No covert at aa?

SKINNER. Not a single part of them concealed.

LADY K. Weill, that's gaun a bit ower faur, there's nae
dout.

SKINNER. It's scandalous.

LADY K. And you're gaun to stop it?

SKINNER. With the help of the presbytery. You don't
mind if I have Kemp and his session clerk along here
to meet me? I left word with his wife that I'd be here,
and that I hoped they'd visit me as soon as Kemp
reached home. I couldn't fix a time to meet him at
the manse, because his wife had no idea when he'd
arrive.

LADY K. It's aa richt, Doctor. Dinna fash. I hae telt ye
ower and ower again: use the hoose as yer ain. Ye're
ane o the faimily.

SKINNER. You make me feel one, certainly. You are very
kind. And how's Kitty? My son tells me we may expect
our first grandchild soon.

LADY K. Oh Kitty's weill eneuch, though whiles gey seik in the mornins, and she gars Joseph pey for it. She's gety wilfou wi him, and I'm shair he's as patient as a saunt. But whiles she gangs ower faur, and he turns moody, and syne she flings oot at him, and bawls the rufe aff, and he gangs white aboot the gills, and sulks, but I daursay they'll improve whan the bairn's born. It's an anxious time.

SKINNER. No doubt. No doubt at all. Perhaps he has business worries?

LADY K. Joseph? Nane that I ken o. Claith's sellin weill, and I think he's talkin o biggin anither shed. I wad say he was thrivin. There's ae thing, though, Doctor.

SKINNER. Oh?

LADY K. I whiles think he looks down his neb at Kitty a wee.

SKINNER. Surely not!

LADY K. It's the wey he's been eddicated, I think.

SKINNER. But he's had no more than the normal school education. He didn't have the brains for college.

LADY K. He has nae lack o brains.

SKINNER. Well, perhaps he lacked the interest.

LADY K. Ye're right there, mebbe, for the ae thing he's interested in is siller, and quite richt tae. But it's the wey ye hae brocht him up to speak, in the English mainner like yersell.

SKINNER. It's the fashion of the future, I'm sure.

LADY K. Mebbe, but it seems to mak him raither critical o Kitty, for whaen she's in her tempers she's gey coorse, juist like her faither, and ye can see it offends his mair refined ear, gin ye can caa it that.

41

SKINNER. You aren't suggesting that he's a little stuck-up, Lady Kilgallon?

LADY K. Weill, I woner, whiles.

SKINNER. It isn't perhaps the boy's own fault, altogether. His mother was a Maule of Panmure.

LADY K. Dr Skinner! Oor Kitty's a Kilgallon o Auchengool!

SKINNER. Oh I'm not condoning his manner. But it's fairly natural that he should have acquired it. His mother had it.

LADY K. I fin it irritatin mysell whiles. Oh I ken I'm naebody. Juist the dochter oa Glesca weaver.

SKINNER. Oh come, Lady Kilgallon.

LADY K. Mind ye, I had a guid eneuch tocher to let me mairry a title, and I like to be treatit like a human bein.

SKINNER. But Joseph doesn't turn his nose up at you!

LADY K. At the wey I speak, mebbe. And if I feel it Kitty will tae, sae I hope ye'll hae a word wi him. Juist tell him it'll mak things a wee thing easier if he minds that there's no muckle faut in no haein taen up the English yet. It's easy eneuch to learn the new weys gin ye bide in Edinburgh, but here in Perth it's weill nigh impossible.

SKINNER. I'll have a word with him. Don't worry.

LADY K. Weill, tak yer chance nou. That was his horse in the stable yaird. Whan he comes in I'll leave ye, to stert the lassies off on the denner, and I'll see that Kitty bides awa tae.

SKINNER. Thank you my dear Lady Kilgallon. It's very considerate of you to confide in me like this, and to give me an opportunity to put matters right.

42

LADY K. Dinna mention it, Doctor. Here he comes.

(Enter JOSEPH SKINNER)

JOSEPH. Oh hullo, father. I didn't know you were coming.

SKINNER. I've come on church affairs. A matter that cropped up suddenly.

LADY K. I'll leave and see the lassies stertit to the denner.

JOSEPH. (To LADY KILGANNON) How's Kitty been today?

LADY K. Gey irritable. Sulkin up in her room. I wadna gang near her yet.

JOSEPH. If you're sure she won't cast it in my teeth that I didn't go up to her at once.

LADY K. I'll tell her yer faither wantit a word wi ye.

SKINNER. It's perfectly true.

LADY K. I'll leave ye.

(She leaves)

JOSEPH. What's wrong?

SKINNER. Oh nothing. Nothing, really. She says Kitty's been flaring up at you occasionally.

JOSEPH. Her condition.

SKINNER. More than that.

JOSEPH. How?

SKINNER. It seems that you sometimes give the impression of being disgusted by the way she speaks.

JOSEPH. Well, father, they do stick here to the old way, when everyone else knows it's finished.

SKINNER. Everyone in polite society in Edinburgh, perhaps. But here in Perth it's still in fashion, so it can't shame you. Don't let it make trouble. Lady Kilgallon's well worth pleasing, my boy. Kilgallon estate may be entailed on Kitty, but her mother can leave her own fortune any way she likes.

JOSEPH. I'm well aware of that, father, and I'm not so sure as I used to be that Kitty will get it, or even our children, should we have them.

SKINNER. What! Surely she hasn't quarrelled with her mother!

JOSEPH. Oh no.

SKINNER. Then have you?

JOSEPH. No, father. But ever since Sir Colin had his last stroke Lady Kilgallon's been growing more and more restless, and now she's started visiting again, alone, and there are rumours that she always turns up where the Earl of Allander's visiting, and leaves with him. He's brought her home here on several occasions lately.

SKINNER. Really! Did they seem more than friendly?

JOSEPH. I couldn't be certain, but he must have felt very friendly to go out of his way so far as to ride home with her.

SKINNER. This is bad news.

JOSEPH. Yes. Sir Colin might pass away any day, and she's young enough to marry again, I suppose.

SKINNER. The Earl isn't likely to be after her money. He's one of the wealthiest men in the country.

JOSEPH. He's a widower and I suppose she's attractive enough.

SKINNER. She can be quite forward.

JOSEPH. Blatantly.

SKINNER. Look here, Joseph, we can't have our hopes
ruined like this. I'll have to contrive something. But I
expect Kemp and his clerk to walk over from the
manse.

(Knocking beyond)

This is probably them. I have a matter to discuss with
them. It won't take me very long. See if you can
arrange to leave me here with your mother-in-law
after they have gone. And see that we aren't disturbed.

JOSEPH. But what can you do, father? Don't please let
her know that I've passed on any gossip.

SKINNER. You know me better than that, surely. Just
leave the whole thing to me.

(KITTY enters)

Oh, here's Kitty.

KITTY. Guid efternune, Doctor. My mither telt me ye
were here. The meenister and the session clerk are
here to see ye. Will I fatch them in here?

SKINNER. Yes, thank you, Kitty. But how are you? Aren't
you going to give your father-in-law a kiss?

JOSEPH. (As she holds up her cheek) I'll fetch Kemp,
father.

(He leaves)

SKINNER. I can't tell you how delighted I am by the news
of the comin event. You're looking very well.

KITTY. I dinna feel it.

SKINNER. Oh, come. Of course, it's a trying time.

KITTY. Ay, and Joseph daesna mak it ony easier. I

45

whiles think he regrets haein mairrit me. He grues at
my Scots tongue.

SKINNER. Ah, yes. But your mother has explained that
little difficulty, and I've had a word with him. You'll
find him much kinder now, I'm sure.

KITTY. I hope sae.

(JOSEPH enters with the REVEREND DAVID KEMP and
ROBIN DOW, his session clerk)

JOSEPH. Your visitors, father.

SKINNER. Ah, Kemp, how are you?

KEMP. Very weill, thank ye. Very weill.

SKINNER. And you, Robin? It is Robin, isn't it? Robin
Dow?

DOW. That's it, juist.

SKINNER. Session clerk. Well, gentlemen, I have work
for you to do, if I can persuade you to see eye to eye
with me.

JOSEPH. We'll leave you, then, father.

KITTY. But will the gentlemen no want some refreshment?

SKINNER. (Sharply) Not now, thank you. Not now. Perhaps
after we have finished our business. But not now. You
agree, gentlemen.

KEMP. Oh, decidedly.

DOW. (Obviously disappointed) Ay, ay, agreed.

SKINNER. Thank you.

(JOSEPH and KITTY leave)

SKINNER. Sit, gentlemen. Have you heard anything here yet of an Italian adventurer called Barocci, who came to Edinburgh last week and tried to stage an exhibition of engravings, of paintings and sculpture from Rome.

KEMP. Rome!

SKINNER. Yes, Rome. Some of them from the Vatican itself.

(Gasps of horror)

Engravings of ceiling paintings and murals. Even a few originals. A painting claiming to be a likeness of Christ Himself, by a Popish painter called Raphael.

KEMP. Na!

SKINNER. Oh but yes, and it was obviously the likeness of some Italian model. Some idle fellow, no doubt, who found posing for an artist less strenuous than honest labour. But you have heard nothing?

KEMP. Na!

DOW. Na!

SKINNER. Then I'm glad I've hurried here to warn you, for young Simon Adair is going to bring Barocci here, to exhibit his pictures in Perth.

KEMP. In Perth!

DOW. Whaur?

SKINNER. That's just where I think you can help, Robin. I'm sure you'll know most of the elders in the presbytery. I thought if you were to seek them out and ask them to keep their ears open, they could report to Mr Kemp here, as the moderator, as soon as they heard of negotiations for the use of premises. You would approve, Mr Kemp?

KEMP. Shairly.

SKINNER. Thank you. Then when you had found where it
was proposed to hold the exhibition you could summon
the proprietor before his kirk session, as we did in
Edinburgh, and threaten him with public denunciation
and loss of communion.

KEMP. There are some gey harde sinners in Perth,
Doctor, men ootside oor Kirk, that could haurdly be
gotten at that way.

SKINNER. Then rouse the multitude against them. Let
every minister in the presbytery use his pulpit to
awaken the people's conscience to the evil of these
pictures. For evil they are. I saw them, and I was
horrified at the effrontery of the men who are giving
this Italian their countenance. Apart from the
sacrilege involved in purporting to represent the
features of our Lord, the nakedness of some of the
figures shown is an affront to modesty and decency.

KEMP. Nakedness?

SKINNER. Yes, nakedness. I tell you, gentlemen, there
are naked men and women in the same pictures as our
Lord and His Mother.

KEMP. Naked althegither?

SKINNER. Some of them, yes.

DOW. Weemen?

SKINNER. Men and women both.

KEMP. In picturs that pretend to show oor Lord!

DOW. Shairly no!

SKINNER. Gentlemen, you have no idea. There were at
least two pictures supposed to be of Mary Magdalen,
and though she wore some clothing it was disarranged,
and (Lowering his voice) her breasts were naked!

KEMP. Na!

48

DOW. Na!

SKINNER. And in several pictures, supposed to be of
Christ's mother, whom you know the Papists worship,
the Holy Child Himself was shown (in a faint whisper)
with his genitals exposed!

KEMP. Sacrilege!

DOW. Filth!

SKINNER. Did you say filth? You know nothing yet.
Besides these so-called religious pictures, which
brazenly violate the second commandment, there are
others of pagan gods and goddesses, and in these the
indecencies beggar description. I saw a picture of
Venus and Mars, and though Mars was fully clothed
in armour, Venus was stark naked, and (Whispering
again) squeezing milk out of one of her breasts with
one hand, while she rested on Mars' shoulder with
the other!

KEMP. And it's proposed to exhibit that in Perth!

SKINNER. My dear Mr Kemp, that is only one of many.
I could go on for an hour recounting horror after
horror, but I am sure you have no desire to be
sickened.

KEMP. If aa this is true, and I dinna dout ye for a meenit,
Doctor, I think we suld caa in the ceevil magistrates
tae. Maist o them are elders, and they wad be
horrified to hear what ye hae juist telt us.

SKINNER. You are quite right, and I thought that as
moderator you might approach the provost.

KEMP. But you hae seen the picturs, Doctor.

SKINNER. Yes, and I shall be very pleased to support
any appeal you make to him, and give my evidence.
Perhaps we could see him together after a meeting
of the presbytery tomorrow afternoon, before I go
to Dundee.

KEMP. Dundee?

SKINNER. After Perth, they intend to stage the exhibition in Dundee. I intend to stop it there too.

KEMP. Ye're greatly to be commended for yer energy in this maitter, Doctor.

SKINNER. Thank you, Mr Kemp. (To DOW) Now you'll remember, Robin, about seeking out the elders, and asking them to keep their eyes and ears open in the town for any sign of an attempt to negotiate the renting of premises.

DOW. Ay ay, Doctor. I'll gang doun into the town the nicht as sune as I hae taen my supper. I left it to hurry oot to Mr Kemp.

KEMP. My meal is waiting too.

SKINNER. Then I shan't keep you.

(He rings a hand bell.
KITTY enters)

Ah, Kitty, we have finished our business now.

KITTY. Will the gentlemen tak some refreshment nou? A stoup o claret, mebbe, or some yill?

SKINNER. They have both left their suppers, and must hurry back for them. Is that not so, gentlemen?

KEMP. Ay, Miss Kitty, thank ye. We maun gang at ance.

DOW. (Crestfallen) Ay, Miss Kitty, thank ye.

KITTY. Some ither time, then, whan ye hae mair leisure.

KEMP. Thank ye. Guid efternune. Shall I caa here for ye on my wey to the meetin the morn, Doctor?

SKINNER. How kind of you, but no. I'll meet you there. I'll be spending the forenoon in the town. Till then,

50

goodbye. Good afternoon, Robin.

DOW. Efternune, Doctor.

(KITTY sees them out.

JOSEPH enters)

JOSEPH. You're finished with them, then?

SKINNER. Yes. Where is your mother-in-law? Still in the kitchen?

JOSEPH. No. She's with Sir Colin. He takes a horrible concoction at this time every day for his heart pains. She has to force him to swallow it.

SKINNER. Does she stay long with him?

JOSEPH. No no. She can't stand the sight of him. She'll be down soon.

SKINNER. Wait here in case Kitty comes back, and remove her.

JOSEPH. Yes.

(KITTY enters)

KITTY. Puir Robin Dow was gey disappeyntit, Doctor, that ye chased him oot withoot ony yill.

SKINNER. He had work to do, and really had to rush.

KITTY. Wad ye like some claret yersell, then?

SKINNER. Well, since my work is over for the day.

KITTY. (To JOSEPH) You?

JOSEPH. (Awkwardly) No thank you. Not yet.

KITTY. (Apeing his accent nastily) Really. (Shrugging) Ah weill.

(She leaves)

SKINNER. What did she mean?

JOSEPH. I suppose she thought it unusual of me to refuse.

SKINNER. Then try to be more natural. But get rid of her.

(Enter LADY KILGALLON)

LADY K. (Lifting her eyes upwards) Did ye hear him?

SKINNER. Sir Colin?

LADY K. Ay. He maks as muckle adae aboot takin his
medicine as a bairn haurdly oot o hippens. Whaur's
Kitty?

SKINNER. She's very kindly gone to fetch me a stoup of
claret.

LADY K. I think I wad like ane tae.

JOSEPH. I'll fetch it.

LADY K. Oh thank ye, Joseph.

(JOSEPH leaves)

He can be a perfect gentleman, whiles.

SKINNER. I'm sorry he doesn't seem to have been
behaving very well lately, but I've had a little talk with
him, and explained that he must be especially
considerate with Kitty just now, and I think you'll find
that he'll improve. We must remember it's their first
child.

LADY K. Ay.

(Enter JOSEPH with two stoups of claret)

JOSEPH. Kitty's going to lie down for a while, and have
her dinner in her room. I said I'd take it up to her.

LADY K. I think she's wyce, and it's kind o ye Joseph.
(Taking stoup) Thank ye.

SKINNER. (Taking stoup) Thank you, Joseph.

JOSEPH. If you'll forgive me, then, I'll see that a tray's
prepared for her.

LADY K. That's a guid laddie.

SKINNER. Go ahead, my boy. I quite understand.

(JOSEPH leaves)

LADY K. My certie, but ye hae made a difference.

SKINNER. A little appeal to his better nature. He's a good
boy, really.

LADY K. Weill, here's to oor first oy.

SKINNER. Oh grandchild, yes.

(They drink)

LADY K. Mind ye, it's a thocht. They say ye never feel
young again.

SKINNER. You mean after becoming a grand-parent. I
wonder. Does it worry you?

LADY K. It daes a wee. I wad hate to feel past it.

SKINNER. Past it. Past what?

LADY K. Life. It's slippin bye me fast the nou, wi this
comin on, and my man gane.

SKINNER. Oh come, come, my lady, not gone.

LADY K. He's feenished as a man, Doctor.

SKINNER. Lady Kilgallon he's still alive.

LADY K. Ye needna be sae mim-moued, Doctor. Ye ken what I mean. And he was a vigorous man in his day. Aye oot and aboot efter deer and hares and muircock, chasin across the country wi his neibor lairds, ridin the wildest horses he could lay his haunds on, and jumpin onything that cam in his wey. He wasna an easy man to thole whiles, but ye couldna say he hadna ony vigour.

SKINNER. A hard drinker, though.

LADY K. Oh, ay, they were a roysterin lot, his freinds hereaboots, and they peyed for it. No mony o them hae lestit. Colin held oot as lang as maist o them, but the drink struck him doun in the end.

SKINNER. You do think it was that?

LADY K. I hae nae dout. Drink's aa richt in moderation, but the wey Colin took it was past aa reason.

SKINNER. It's a great pity. And very hard on you. You certainly are too young to be left without a, eh, healthy partner.

LADY K. I dae feel it whiles, Doctor. (In a burst of confidence) There are times I feel sae restless I can haurdly contain mysell.

SKINNER. We all have our struggles, Lady Kilgallon, and I'm sure you are no exception. For a woman so personable there must be constant temptations.

LADY K. Temptations?

SKINNER. There must be men in the neighbourhood who admire you, and are not too scrupulous to make advances.

LADY K. (Flattered) Oho, hae ye been hearin stories?

SKINNER. Me? No. Has someone been making advances to you?

LADY K. Dear me no. At least, no in ony wey that ye
could caa offensive. The Earl o Allander's ridden
hame wi me ance or twice frae Leddy Mary Drummond's
but I didna think ocht o it. He's no a man I tak to. Ower
auld and scraggy to be muckle o a gallant, and raither
effeminate in his mainners. He daesna appeal to me.

SKINNER. You seem to appeal to him, though. I must say
I can't quarrel with his taste.

LADY K. (Coyly) Oh, Doctor.

SKINNER. I do think you should be careful not to encourage
him, though, under the circumstances. It might look
as though you were anticipating, eh, a certain, eh,
event, eh, an event which happens to all of us sooner
or later, and to some of us sooner than others.

LADY K. (Bluntly) This is his third stroke, Doctor. He
can haurdly survive anither.

SKINNER. No. And I suppose it is only natural that you
should consider possibilities, and look ahead.

LADY K. Nou Doctor, the thocht's haurdly crossed my
mind. And if ye're thinking I could be content wi the
like o the Earl o Allander I declare ye misjudge me
sairly. I swer I haena gien the idea a thocht. But as
ye said yersell I'm young to be left withoot a, eh,
healthy man, and whan an eligible bachelor peys me
mair nor ordinar attention I canna deny that it
quickens my bluid a wee. It, weill, it shows me I
still hae a chance.

SKINNER. You need have no doubt on that score, I assure
you.

LADY K. Dae ye think sae?   (Quite directly) Dae ye fin
me attractive, Doctor?

SKINNER. My dear lady, that is something I have no right
to tell you.

LADY K. What wey no?

SKINNER. You are a married woman, Lady Kilgallon, and
I am a minister of the Church.

LADY K. Suppose for a meenit that I was a weeda, and you
were a lawyer or a doctor. Wad ye fin me attractive?

SKINNER. Well, I really have no right to tell you.

LADY K. Come on.

SKINNER. (As though outmanoeuvred) You make my
position very difficult, Phemie. You know I find you
attractive.

LADY K. You caeed me Phemie.

SKINNER. It was a slip of the tongue. Forgive me. I had
no right to be so familiar.

LADY K. But ye dae fin me attractive?

SKINNER. (As though resenting having to make the
admission) Yes.

LADY K. You're no that auld aither, Doctor. Dae ye no
miss mairrit life, for aa ye're a minister?

SKINNER. (As though struggling against surrender) Yes,
I tell you.

LADY K. We could comfort ane anither.

SKINNER. Don't tempt me. It would be wrong.

LADY K. It wad dae naebody ony hairm.

SKINNER. Your husband.

LADY K. Ye could tell him to his face and it wad mean
naething. He's juist an object. An object.

SKINNER. (Insincerely) Surely not.

LADY K. I need a man, Samuel.

SKINNER. The children.

LADY K. They needna ken.

SKINNER. (Suddenly afraid they will be interrupted before they have arrived at an understanding) I hear someone!

LADY K. (Whispering suddenly) The nicht! I'll come to yer room!

SKINNER. Ssh!

(Enter JOSEPH)

LADY K. Oh it's you, Joseph. Hou's Kitty?

JOSEPH. She's going to try to sleep now. Dinner's ready. Are you coming?

LADY K. (To SKINNER) Ay, come.

(She gives him her arm. JOSEPH follows them out, wondering.)

ACT THREE

(The Bridge End Tavern, near Perth. Door from road. Door to kitchen and courtyard under stairs leading to upper rooms.

NEIL BELL discovered lifting pewter stoups from one of the tables. SIMON ADAIR comes downstairs, followed by BAROCCI.)

SIMON. Oh, Neil.

NEIL. Ay, Maister?

SIMON. My friend's cases. You've had them put where they can come to no harm?

NEIL. They're through at the back o the yaird.

SIMON. Under cover?

NEIL. In the barn.

SIMON. They won't have to be moved until he needs them, I hope ?

NEIL. Weill na, Maister, as lang as he needs them afore the back end. The barn'll be tuim till hairst.

SIMON. He'll need them within a few days, I expect. Until then, you'll see that no one touches them?

NEIL. Shairly, Maister.

SIMON. Come then, Barocci, and I'll introduce you to

Perth. (As they leave) The people are no more tolerant here than in Edinburgh, but my father has considerable influence, since his estate borders the town, and we may not be repulsed.

(QUEENIE comes downstairs just as they disappear)

NEIL. Are their rooms in order.

QUEENIE. Ay, faither. I woner at the young Maister bidin here, whan he could juist hae gane hame to the castle.

NEIL. To be wi his freind, likely.

QUEENIE. He could shairly hae taen his freind to the castle tae.

NEIL. Ay, but his freind has aa thae cases. He's mebbe come to dae some kind o business wi them in the toun.

QUEENIE. He winna hae cast oot wi his faither, think ye?

NEIL. The Maister!

QUEENIE. He mebbe daesna like the idea o his faither making a fule o himsell wi Leddy Kilgallon.

NEIL. Ye suldna cairry clash, lassie. What though he's ridden hame wi her ance or twice draw a freind's hoose? It's hus guid mainners. Her ain man's no able to tak her aboot nou, and nae gentleman wad see her ride hame alane.

QUEENIE. She rides oot alane.

NEIL. That's different.

QUEENIE. I dout it's mair nor juist clash, faither.

NEIL. It's queer ye suld be sae shair o it, for Sir Colin's groom was in this mornin, on his wey to the smiddy, and he had a different tale to tell.

QUEENIE. And what did he say?

NEIL. Weill, Queenie, ye ken the rule in oor tred. Ye
hear aa, but ye tell nocht.

QUEENIE. Sae ye think I canna be trustit?

NEIL. Na na, but it's an unco tale, and Tam Weir suld hae
haen mair sense nor to pass it on, for it could cost
him his job.

QUEENIE. Oot wi it, faither. What was it?

NEIL. He said ane o the Auchengool lassies saw Leddy
Kilgallon comin oot o a guest's room juist as it was
growin licht the ither mornin.

QUEENIE. A guest's? Ye mean a man's? Some man that
was bidin there?

NEIL. Ay, and what man, think ye? Her ain dochter's
guid-faither. Him that used to be minister o
Auchengool afore Mr. Kemp.

QUEENIE. Dr. Skinner! I dinna believe it!

NEIL. That's what Tam Weir said.

QUEENIE. Ye ken Tam Weir. He wad say onything aboot
Leddy Kilgallon. Ye ken hou she yokit on to him aboot
smugglin drink ben to Sir Colin. It's juist spite,
faither.

NEIL. Na na. I ken Tam Weir hates her, but I dinna
blame him. He's Sir Colin's man, and he juist has to dae
what Sir Colin tells him. And I'm shair he's as
truithfou as maist.

QUEENIE. But Dr Skinner! Wi a wumman in his room!
Faither, it juist isna possible, for Mr Kemp was
sayin in his sermon yesterday that it was Dr Skinner
that stoppit some Italian in Edinburgh frae showin aff a
lot of filthy picturs wi nakit weemen in them. That
daesna soond like a man that wad commit adultery.
Forbye, he's a meenister.

NEIL. Did ye say an Italian?

QUEENIE. An Italian.

NEIL. Did ye say he stoppit an Italian frae showin his picturs?

QUEENIE. Ay.

NEIL. Mr Kemp said this?

QUEENIE. Ay yesterday, they say, in Auchengool kirk. And he said the Italian was comin to Perth, to try the same thing there, and the folk suld band thegither and drive the man furth o the toun.

NEIL. But Queenie, the Maister and his freind!

QUEENIE. Oh ay, his freind!

NEIL. Italian!

QUEENIE. Foreign, onywey.

NEIL. Italian, there's nae dout! And thae cases I had putten awa in the barn for him!

QUEENIE. The picturs, think ye?

NEIL. I dout sae.

QUEENIE. But the young Maister wad hae naething to dae wi onything filthy, faither. I'm shair o that. There's naething I dinna ken aboot the men that caa here, and there's nae man mair to be trustit to behave like a gentleman whan ye fin yersell alane wi him than oor ain young Maister.

NEIL. I wad hae thocht that.

QUEENIE. Then ye jalouse that the picturs arena filthy efter aa?

NEIL. Wha kens.

(Distant murmuration of the crowd. They drift to the
door looking out on the road)

There's a pairty on the brig.

QUEENIE. There's a lot o them!

NEIL. (As the sound increases) Provost Drummond!

QUEENIE. And Beylie Hay!

NEIL. And Kemp himsell !

QUEENIE. And ilka man o the toun watch!

NEIL. And a rabble at their heels! I woner what this
means. Mischief, by the look o it. Queenie, rin oot to
the yaird and fin ane o the ostlers, ony o them, and gar
him ride hell for leather for Mungo Meikle, the Earl's
baron beylie, and tell him we need help. Say the toun
magistrates are here to usurp his authority. That'll
fetch him.

QUEENIE. (Leaving hurriedly by the back door) Ay,
faither.

(The murmuration increases. Enter PROVOST
DRUMMOND, BAILIE HAY, the REVEREND DAVID
KEMP, ROBIN DOW, and several others, including
members of the town watch with halberds, who take up
positions at the doors.)

NEIL. Ay Provost? Ye look as if there's something the
maitter. Are ye efter somebody?

PROVOST. Hae ye ony foreigners bidin here?

NEIL. There's naebody bidin here the nou bune the young
Maister o Allander and a freind o his frae Edinburgh.

PROVOST. Is the freind foreign?

NEIL. I dinna ken. I neir thocht o speirin.

KEMP. Ye need hae nae dout, Provost. It was the Maister
   o Allander that brocht the Italian ower here frae Rome.

(Growl at the mention of Rome)

PROVOST. Are they in the hoose the nou?

NEIL. They gaed oot ower to the toun no twa meenits syne.
   It's a woner ye didna meet them.

PROVOST. Whilk rooms hae they?

NEIL. What wey?

PROVOST. I'm gaun to hae them lookit.

NEIL. Ye hae nae jurisdiction here, Provost. Whan ye
   cross that brig to come ower here ye're ower the toun
   boonds and into Allander estate. The Earl's baron
   beylie's the authority here.

PROVOST. (Ignoring this) Beylie Hay.

HAY. Ay, Provost?

PROVOST. Tak twa o yer men and hae a guid look through
   their rooms.

NEIL. Ye daurna.

PROVOST. Dae what ye're telt, Beylie.

HAY. (Worried) What will the Earl say?

KEMP. What can he say? He canna uphauld idolatry.

HAY. But we hae nae authority on his grun.

KEMP. The presbytery has authority in speeritual
   maitters ower the haill county. This is a speeritual
   maitter. And you're an elder o the kirk, forbye.

PROVOST. (to HAY) Dae what ye're telt.

HAY. But if we touch their property.

KEMP. Filthy abominations! (Growl) The presbytery wants them destroyed.

HAY. But the presbytery sauld ask the baron beylie to destroy them.

KEMP. Him! And his maister neist door to a Papist! Ye ken he still keeps the auld curate at the castle, that had Allander pairish afore the Revolution. We suld hurry, Provost, afore the Maister and his Italian freind come back.

PROVOST. (To HAY) Are ye gaun to look through their rooms, Beylie, or will I hae to dae it mysell?

(Murmuration from beyond the door. 'Come on, Beylie. On wi it. Ay, on wi it. He's feart.' etc.)

HAY. (To NEIL) Whilk rooms hae they?

PROVOST. (As NEIL remains silent) Look through them aa.

HAY. (To the men of the town watch) Keep haudin the doors. Willie. Jock. You come wi me.

(The three march up the stairs. They have no sooner gone out of sight than there is a yelling outside the front door and shortly afterwards SIMON ADAIR enters with BAROCCI, to be stopped by the guards. BAROCCI looks dishevelled and terrified. Outside cries can be heard: 'Papist! Idolator! Anti'Christ!')

PROVOST. (To guards) Let them bye.

(They stagger forward)

SIMON. Provost Drummond! What do you mean by this? Mr Kemp, what are you doing here? What's going on, Neil?

NEIL. Beylie Hay's awa up the stair wi twa o the toun

watch. I could dae naething to stop them.

SIMON. But they have no jurisdiction here!

NEIL. Juist what I telt them.

SIMON. You should have sent for Mungo Meikle.

NEIL. I did juist that, Maister, the meenit I saw this rabble comin.

(Growls of anger)

SIMON. Good man. On a fast horse, I hope.

NEIL. Ay, Maister.

SIMON. Well, Provost, what do you mean by this demonstration? Or have I you to thank, Mr Kemp? Do you know that the rabble outside has used threatening language to my friend? They even laid hands on him, the scoundrels. Look at his clothes.

PROVOST. Ye suld hae kent better nor fetch yer freind here, sir.

SIMON. Why should I not bring my friend here? Why should I not take my friend anywhere I like? What has my friend done to be treated like this? (As BAILIE HAY re-appears) Ah, Bailie Hay, where have you been? What have you been up to? Have you dared to interfere with our baggage?

HAY. I was telt to gang through it by the Provost, Maister.

SIMON. How often have you been told, Bailie, that your jurisdiction is confined to the town.

KEMP. This is a speeritual maitter, Maister. Allandale estate's in the boonds o Perth presbytery.

SIMON. There's nothing spiritual about rifling people's property. I ask you again, Bailie. Have you interfered with our baggage?

PROVOST. (To HAY) Did ye fin what ye were efter?

HAY. Na, juist claes.

PROVOST. Then the picturs are somewhaur else. (To NEIL) Had they ony baggage that isna in their rooms?

SIMON. You're exceeding your duty, Provost.

PROVOST. Am I? Is it no yer freind's intention to exhibit thae picturs in Perth?

SIMON. Of course it's his intention. And why not? They're great works of art.

(Angry murmuration, growing to an outcry)

KEMP. (Crying loudly) Great works of sacrilege! Inducements to idolatry! Filthy and indecent likenesses of naked men and women! Perverted atrocities!

(Great cheer from beyond the door. Ominous pressure on the guards)

NEIL. This is my hoose. I warn ye, Provost. Keep oot the rabble.

PROVOST. The gairds are daein their best. Beylie Hay, tak yer twa men ootbye and tak a look through the biggins aboot the yaird.

SIMON. Keep all your men here, Bailie Hay, and help to guard the front door, for I warn you that if the rabble is allowed in, and anyone is injured, or any property damaged, I shall hold you responsible.

PROVOST. (To HAY) Dae what ye're telt, Beylie.

HAY. (To his two helpers) Come on.

(He leads them out through the back door. Just as they go the murmuration of the crowd outside grows again and swells by the front door. Voices are heard: 'Mak wey there. Mak wey for the Baron Beylie. Mak wey for the Baron Beylie. 'The murmuration dies almost to a silence.

MUNGO MEIKLE enters, parting the two front door guards with his broadsword. He is followed by several armed men, all of whom immediately take up positions beside the guards of the town watch. Besides their broadswords they carry pistols in their belts, whereas of the town contingent only the PROVOST has a pistol.)

SIMON. Thank God you have come, Mungo.

MUNGO. (A great mountain of a man) Hae they as muckle as laid a haund on ye?

SIMON. No, but Bailie Hay has gone through our baggage.

MUNGO. Whaur is he?

SIMON. Out in the yard, searching for some cases of pictures which belong to my friend. I'm afraid that if they find them they will damage them. They are precious.

(Growls, silenced by a scowl from MUNGO MEIKLE)

MUNGO. Hou mony men has he oot there wi him?

SIMON. Two.

MUNGO. Airmed?

SIMON. Beilie Hay has a broadsword. His men have halberds.

MUNGO. (To one of his men) Order Beylie Hay to come in here at ance. If he resists, present yer pistol. Tell him ye'll blaw his heid aff.

(The man leaves by the back door)

I'm surprised at ye, Provost, lendin yer coontenance to sic lawless ongauns. As for you, Mr Kemp, I hae nae dout you're at the bottom o the haill affair. I hear ye

preached a sermon yesterday, incitin yer congregation
to destroy this gentleman's picturs, whan he brocht
them to Perth.

PROVOST. He winna show them in Perth. That's a
certainty.

MUNGO. Mebbe no, but till they get to Perth you'll leave
them alane.

KEMP. This estate is within the boonds o the presbytery.
The presbytery has ordert their destruction.

MUNGO. Through the toun Magistrates? Whan they're on
Allander estate? That's a wee thing irregular, Mr
Kemp.

KEMP. Then in the name o the presbytery I order you to
seek them oot and destroy them.

MUNGO. But ye hae heard what the Maister says. They
belang to his freind.

(Enter MUNGO's MESSENGER leading in BAILIE HAY
and his two helpers)

PROVOST. (To HAY) Did ye fin what ye were efter?

HAY. Ay, they're in the barn, in wuiden cases.

MUNGO. (To two of his men at the back door) Fin them and
gaird them, you twa. (As the men leave) I was
speirin at ye, Beylie Hay. What dae ye mean by
usurpin my authority?

PROVOST. He was cairryin oot my orders.

MUNGO. And what richt had you to order him to interfere
wi ony man's property on Allander estate? Dae ye no
ken that I could hae ye disairmed this meenit and flung
in the castle pit, for brawlin on the Earl's grun? Ye're
mebbe cock o the midden ower that brig, Provost, but
here ye're naebody, and the suner ye tak Baylie Hay
and yer toun watch furth o the tavern here, and back

ower the brig, the better for ye.

PROVOST. Aa richt. Aa richt. But I warn the Maister: let his freind juist try to bring thae filthy picturs ower the brig, and they'll brunt at the cross. And what's mair, his freind'll leave the toun astride a stang.

SIMON. The pictures aren't filthy.

KEMP. Filthy, sacrilegious and idolatrous!

SIMON. Nonsense. You know nothing about them.

PROVOST. We were telt aa aboot them by Dr Skinner.

SIMON. But you haven't seen them for yourselves.

KEMP. Can ye deny that they pretend to portray Jesus Christ? Can ye deny that they show nakit men and weemen?

(Growls from beyond the front door)

SIMON. They are engravings of famous paintings. Great works of art.

KEMP. Papish abominations.

SIMON. Popish, yes. But great works of art.

KEMP. Ye see, he admits it. Papish.

PROVOST. (Sarcastic) Oh but the Maister thinks there's naething wrang wi bein Papish. He's next door to a Papist himsell.

SIMON. I'm an Episcopalian.

(Growls)

KEMP. The evil is in oor ain midst.

MUNGO. (Infuriated) What did ye say? Episcopalian? Evil? Mr Kemp, and you tae, Provost, I hae warnt ye that I could hae ye arrestit for brawlin on the Earl's grun. Will ye tak yersell aff at ance, afore I order my men to grip ye?

PROVOST. (With hand touching pistol) Juist you daur.

MUNGO. Oho, eh! (Drawing his pistol) Ye wad cock yer groset at me, Provost Drummond.

(Provoking him by poking him with the point of the broadsword.)

Ye wad drae yer pistol, mebbe, and shute me, if I laid haunds on ye?

(The PROVOST takes his hand from his pistol)

It's primed, is it?

(He prises it out of the PROVOST's belt with the point of the broadsword, so that it falls to the floor. The PROVOST jumps in alarm.

Oho, eh! Ye thocht it micht gan aff, did ye, and blaw yer taes aff? See here, Provost, oot wi ye! (To the whole town contingent) Oot wi ye! Oot wi the lot o ye!

(MUNGO and his men press against the town contingent and persuade them out through the front door)

KEMP. Mair will be heard o this. The last word hasna yet been spoken.

MUNGO Your last word'll sune hae been spoken, gin ye dinna haud yer tongue! (As he leaves) Come on, ower the brig wi ye! The haill lot o ye! G'on, ye useless rabble! On wi ye, gin ye dinna want some reid-het leid in yer hin-ends!

(The murmuration of the crowd recedes into the distance)

SIMON. Thank God they've gone.

SIGNOR. What people. None of them have seen my pictures. Yet they want to destroy them.

NEIL. I think yer freind could dae wi a dram, Maister. I hae French brandy and Hollands gin.

SIMON. Brandy, Barocci?

SIGNOR. Si, I thank you.

SIMON. (To NEIL) For me too.

NEIL. Brandy for the twa gentlemen, Queenie.

QUEENIE. Ay, faither.

(She leaves by the back door)

NEIL. I'll juist see that yer freind's cases are safe and sound, Maister.

SIMON. Do, Neil.

(NEIL follows QUEENIE)

SIGNOR. This is the finish. I have wasted my time and my money. I go back to England. To London.

SIMON. Perth does seem to be out of the question.

SIGNOR. They say they will burn my pictures at a cross. Why at a cross?

SIMON. A market cross. They have a stone cross where they hold their market. It's the most frequented part of the town, where they make all proclamations.

SIGNOR. And burn pictures they have never seen.

SIMON. They certainly threatened to do so. Yes, Barocci, Perth is off.

SIGNOR. And the other town, Dundee.

SIMON. Oh no, we must try Dundee. It will be different.

SIGNOR. Different? From Edinburgh? From Perth?

SIMON. Ah yes, for in Edinburgh we had the bad luck to encounter Dr Skinner. And by chance he had connections with Perth also. He used to be the minister of a parish here. But as far as I know he has no connections with Dundee.

(NEIL returns)

Are the cases all right, Neil?

NEIL. Ay, and twa o Mungo's men are still on gaird, and'll bide there till he caas them aff.

(QUEENIE enters)

Thank ye, Queenie. (Taking the brandy from her) Yer brandy, gentlemen.

(QUEENIE lingers by the back door as he serves them)

SIGNOR. Thank you.

SIMON. Thank you, Neil. I have been telling Signor Barocci not to lose heart. Perth is out of the question, but he may have more luck in Dundee, for all the trouble has been caused by Dr. Skinner, and as far as I know he has no connections there. You will know him well, Neil. He held Auchengool parish before Mr Kemp. Where had he been before that?

NEIL. He cam to Auchengool frae a pairish up in Angus, but if it's Dr Skinner that's fashin ye, ye needna gie the man anither thocht, Maister. Queenie, tak some yill oot to the twa gairds in the yaird, and hae some mair ready for Mungo's ither men whan they come back.

QUEENIE. (Understanding what her father is after) Ay, faither.

72

(She leaves by the back door)

NEIL. I had to get her oot o the wey, Maister. It's no a maitter for a young lassie to hear. But yer freind Dr Skinner...

SIMON. He's no friend of mine.

NEIL. Na, nor o mine aither. I aye kent he was a hypocrite. Nou it's a thing I wadna talk aboot for ordinar, but seein the man's fashin ye, and ye're in dout as to what to dae neist, I think it's mebbe my duty to yer faither's son to tell ye that Leddy Kilgallon was seen comin oot o Dr. Skinner's room the ither mornin, juist afore it grew licht.

SIMON. No! Who says so?

NEIL. Sir Colin's groom, Tam Weir. An honest man if ever there was ane.

SIMON. He seems to carry tales out of his employer's house, though.

NEIL. Weill, mebbe, but withoot ony disloyalty to Sir Colin.

SIMON. In any case what has this story got to do with my friend Signor Barocci's plans?

NEIL. It micht hae a lot to dae wi his plans Maister, for Tam Weir thocht it his duty to let his maister ken hou the land lay.

SIMON. That was making mischief, with a vengeance.

NEIL. Weill, there was mebbe guid eneuch excuse, Maister, for my leddy was whiles gey sair on him for peyin mair heed to Sir Colin's orders than to her ain, and what wey suld he no, and him Sir Colin's groom?

SIMON. But if Sir Colin is so enfeebled in mind and body that he has to be looked after like a child, perhaps Lady Kilgallon is the correct person to issur orders, even to Sir Colin's personal servants.

NEIL. Weill, mebbe sae, I dinna ken. But the fact is that
Tam Weir telt Sir Colin aboot his wife gaun to Dr
Skinner's room, and the upshot was that Sir Colin gart
Tam fetch the factor, and gart the factor send for his
lawyer.

SIMON. Divorce!

NEIL. Juist that, though ye maunna let on I telt ye.

SIMON. You need have no fear, I assure you. Besides, I
simply can't believe you.

NEIL. Nou Maister...

SIMON. I mean, I simply can't believe that Sir Colin's
groom wasn't mistaken. There may have been some
quite innocent explanation of the whole thing.

NEIL. Wi Dr Skinner! I dout it. It's no the first time there
hae been rumours. He has a reputation...

SIMON. I know. The Widows' Friend. But this amounts to
a charge of adultery. And divorce. It would ruin him.

NEIL. There's nae dout.

SIMON. And it would rebound on Sir Colin's own family.
He has his daughter to consider, married to Skinner's
son. No, no, I'm sure Sir Colin will be prevailed upon
to think twice. That is, if the story's true.

NEIL. I'm shair it's true.

SIMON. Even so, I'm sure Sir Colin was simply giving vent
to his anger. He'll never press for divorce. It would
be foolish.

NEIL. Ye canna be shair.

SIMON. His factor will probably humour him, and let the
matter drop, or even put the matter in the hands of

74

Lady Kilgallon herself, if Sir Colin is as bad as they say.

NEIL. He wasna sae bad that he didna flee aff the haunle, onywey.

SIMON. It will come to nothing.

NEIL. Mebbe, but will Dr Skinner ken that? Dae ye no think the fear o the haill maitter being made public'll gar him want to lie low for a while?

SIMON. If Lady Kilgallon was seen coming out of his room.

NEIL. (Beginning to show offence) I dinna dout Tam Weir's word.

SIMON. Very well, you may be right, and Dr Skinner may be in no position to make further trouble for my friend here. You understand, Signor Barocci, what we have been discussing?

SIGNOR. Si, yes. Dr Skinner can now say nothing against my pictures, because ha had another man's wife in his room.

SIMON. That's what it amounts to, yes. So you see, Barocci, you mustn't give in. We must go on to Dundee.

SIGNOR. Simon, I am sorry, but I cannot afford another loss, and I cannot risk my Raphael, or my Titian, or my Tintoretto. They are too precious to be burnt at a cross.

SIMON. But this time there will be no Dr Skinner.

SIGNOR. Perhaps no Dr Skinner. But another Scotch priest, is it minister you name them? Your Mr what is his name, Kemp? Another of him, perhaps. Another crowd of people, is it rabble you name it? More yelling and screaming and saying filthy, and sacrilege, and idolatry? No, Simon, my friend.

SIMON. Giorgio, don't you realise how wrong it is to give

in to this sort of thing? We have to make a stand or we are allowing these dullards to prevail, to impose their standards on all around them. We must go on until a sufficient number of open-minded and intelligent people have seen the beauty of what we have to offer, to ensure that the ignorant and bigoted will never again go unopposed. We have a duty, Giorgio. A duty to Scotland.

SIGNOR. You may have a duty to your country, Master Simon, but I have a duty to my pictures. They must not be destroyed.

SIMON. They have not really been in any danger.

SIGNOR. If your father's great Mungo had not arrived...

SIMON. But he did.

SIGNOR. Si, yes, but just in time.

SIMON. Yes, but there won't be the same trouble at Dundee.

SIGNOR. How do I know? And there is the expense of the journey, perhaps for nothing. And I have been at the expense of the journey here, and to Scotland, and all for nothing.

SIMON. Giorgio, I will guarantee you against loss out of my own pocket. I will pay the expenses of the Dundee journey. And we can go most of the way by boat, down the firth, and stay on board until we are sure of a favourable reception. Will a boat be available, think you, Neil?

NEIL. I wad think sae.

(A slight commotion)

SIMON. Or wait. This sounds like Mungo.

(MUNGO enters, alone)

MUNGO. They're awa back ower the brig, Maister, and I

hae telt my men to watch the brig-end till I caa them
aff. Ye need hae nae fear mou o ony bother, but I wad
advise ye to move oot o here the nicht.

SIMON. Just what we were discussing. Brandy, Mungo, or
gin?

MUNGO. Yill, if ye please, Maister.

SIMON. Yes ale, Neil.

NEIL. Ay, Maister.

(He leaves)

SIMON. Mungo, can you find a boat to take us down the
firth to Dundee, with our baggage and my friend's
cases?

MUNGO. Ay, Maister, there's a lugger in the nou frae
Broughty Ferry, and the skipper's aff yer faither's
estate, ane Jock Wylie.

SIMON. Can his business here wait?

MUNGO. Hoot ay, for onything you want, Maister.

SIMON. Find out.

MUNGO. Ay, Maister, and I'll see the cases loadid, and
the twa o ye safely on board.

(NEIL enters)

NEIL. Yer yill, Mungo.

MUNGO. Thank ye. Yer health, gentlemen.

SIMON. (Raising his glass) To success in Dundee.

(BAROCCI gives a wry look)

Yes, Barocci, success. Raise your glass, man and
keep up your courage.

(BAROCCI raises his glass, like a condemned man. MUNGO drinks off the contents of his stoup without drawing a breath)

MUNGO. (Putting down his empty stoup) I'll see Jock Wylie aboot his lugger nou, Maister. The suner the better.

SIMON. (Rising) Thank you.

(MUNGO leaves)

Can you have a meal ready in half an hour, Neil?

NEIL. Gin ye'll tak beylt ham or cauld reist mutton, or I could gie ye smokies dune in milk.

SIMON. Lay out what you have.

NEIL. Ay, Maister.

(He leaves)

SIMON. Come, Barocci, let us check our baggage.

SIGNOR. We go to Dundee?

SIMON. Yes, by boat.

SIGNOR. I am not happy.

SIMON. Oh come, Giorgio, you will cheer up when you find that our luck has turned. And remember, I will bear any loss.

SIGNOR. (Shrugging apologetically) If not, I cannot continue.

SIMON. I understand.

(They go upstairs. NEIL enters and starts to lay the table. QUEENIE enters to help)

QUEENIE. Did ye say they were gaun on to Dundee, faither?

NEIL. Ay.

QUEENIE. Thae twa men that Beylie Hay had oot in the yaird wi him.

NEIL. Ay?

QUEENIE. They were talkin aboot Dr Skinner.

NEIL. Ay?

QUEENIE. Ane o them said he suld hae been there wi the Provost, but the ither ane said he couldna, because he had to set oot for Dundee as sune as he had spoken to the presbytery here.

NEIL. God, the man isna blate! Awa to dae the Lord's wark in Dundee, efter touslin wi Leddy Kilgallon.

QUEENIE. Mebbe he daesna ken she was seen leavin his room.

NEIL. Mebbe ye're richt.

QUEENIE. Suld ye no warn the Maister, faither, that Dr Skinner's in Dundee?

NEIL. Na, lassie. Say nocht to a sowl. That rabble was gey wild the day, and Mungo Meikle himsell was fasht a wee, or he wadna hae advised the Maister to slip awa frae here efter daurk. Na na, lassie, I'm a loyal Allander tenant, but I'll hae nae peace o mind till that Italian and his picturs are weill awa frae this Tavern. Sae see to the haddies, and haud yer tongue.

QUEENIE. Ay, faither.

ACT FOUR

(MRS LUCY LINDSAY's flat in the Lawnmarket. JENNY
GILLIES opens the landing door and ushers in LORD
KILMARDINNY)

JENNY. I dinna think she'll be lang, my lord. Will ye tak
a sait?

KILMARDINNY. Thank ye, Jenny.

JENNY. (Going to the door of the inner room, knocking,
and opening it) Lord Kilmardinny's here, mem.

(JENNY returns to the hall door as MRS LINDSAY
enters from the inner room)

LUCY. Good afternoon, uncle Tom. (She holds up her
cheek to be kissed) I didn't expect you today. I under-
stood you were busy.

KILMARDINNY. I'm aye that, but I hae news for ye.

LUCY. From Jamaica?

KILMARDINNY. Frae Fairbairn and Witherspune. I telt
ye they had opent up a brainch oot there.

LUCY. Yes. You were going to instruct them to act for
me.

KILMARDINNY. Juist that. I askit them to keep an ee on
yer man, to see if he was behavin himsell. Weill, he
isna.

LUCY. Some other woman! She must think very little of her reputation. He's still a married man.

KILMARDINNY. She has nae reputation to think o, lassie. She's daurk.

LUCY. Black!

KILMARDINNY. Ay.

LUCY. Surely not! Really! Only once, or does he make a habit of it?

KILMARDINNY. He maks mair nor a habit o it. In this country she wad be his lowfou wife.

LUCY. You mean he lives with her?

KILMARDINNY. Mair or less. They hae twa bairns.

LUCY. Oh uncle Tom, no!

KILMARDINNY. I dout sae.

LUCY. And you have proof of all this?

KILMARDINNY. I hae askit for sworn testimony.

LUCY. Then I can get a divorce.

KILMARDINNY. Weill, we'll hae soond legal grund, but I wadna advise it. It's an affront, lassie, his leavin ye and takin up wi a wumman like that, and a divorce wad juist draw attention to it.

LUCY. But uncle Tom, I want my freedom.

KILMARDINNY. What wey that? (Suspiciously) Hae ye someane in mind?

LUCY. No, I just want my freedom.

KILMARDINNY. There is someane, Lucy. Oot wi it. Wha is it?

LUCY. Uncle Tom, there's nobody. I just want to be free of that man.

KILMARDINNY. He'll no bother ye, I'll wager, and if he daes ye can aye tell him that we ken aa.

LUCY. I want to be free of him.

KILMARDINNY. Think, lassie, o the disgrace o haein it brocht oot in coort. And I dinna want to seem selfish, but ye hae me to think o tae, Lucy.

LUCY. I know, uncle Tom, but surely nobody will think less of you because you have a niece who was misguided enough to marry a rotter.

KILMARDINNY. It isna that, Lassie. It's what he left ye for.

LUCY. Surely if I don't mind it being known you shouldn't. Though it will give spiteful people a chance to laugh, I admit.

KILMARDINNY. There's nae dout, and if I were you, lassie, I wad think aboot it. See here, suppose ye leave it like this, that if somane comes alang ye feel ye can settle doun wi, and ye feel he's interested in you, ye can let faa a hint that ye can get a divorce gin ye want it, wi nae bother at aa. Sall we leave it at that, eh?

LUCY. But you'll have to go on supporting me, uncle Tom. If I had a divorce I'd surely be granted my pensions again.

KILMARDINNY. I hae been to the twa faculties. The procurators think the wey I dae, that the haill maitter wad be better keepit quait, and they're willin to help ye again.

LUCY. By the same amount?

KILMARDINNY. By mair. Twall pounds insteid o eicht. They acknowledge that things are growing dearer.

LUCY. And the surgeons?

KILMARDINNY. The same as afore.

LUCY. Uncle Tom, it's really very generous of them.

KILMARDINNY. Ay ay, no bad. And dinna think for a
meenit because the procurators are gaun to be mair
generous that I'll reduce the allouance I used to mak.

LUCY. Oh uncle Tom, you're too kind.

KILMARDINNY. Na na, I can weill afford it, and if ye keep
the haill thing quait ye'll be pleasin me tae, and to tell
ye the truith if ye're gaun to mairry again I wad like to
be weill eneuch aff to be able to tak some time to mak
up yer mind, and no be forced to jump at the first man
that cam alang wi eneuch siller to keep ye.

LUCY. Oh uncle Tom, I'd never think of giving myself to
any man just for his money.

KILMARDINNY. Ye could dae waur.

LUCY. You don't mean it.

KILMARDINNY. Weill, ye did ance afore.

LUCY. Uncle Tom, that's mean.

KILMARDINNY. Mebbe ay.

LUCY. And it's silly. One would think by the way you're
talking that I was suddenly going to be sought after by
every man I met. I'm a lot older than I used to be.
I doubt very much whether, even if I did get a divorce
and was known to be free to marry, any man would
look at me.

KILMARDINNY. I ken ane that wad jump at ye gey quick,
gin he wasna yer uncle.

LUCY. Oh uncle Tom, you're so good for my spirits.
Shall I tell you a secret?

KILMARDINNY. What?

LUCY. If you weren't my uncle, I would jump at you too.

KILMARDINNY. Wad ye?

LUCY. Yes.

(She kisses him, almost wantonly. He suddenly becomes uncomfortable)

KILMARDINNY. Lassie, this isna richt. I say fulish things whiles. I'd better gang.

LUCY. Oh uncle Tom, have I been forward?

KILMARDINNY. Not a bit. I hae been juist a wee thing blunt aboot my feelins, and they're feelins I'm not supposed to hae.

(Knock)

LUCY. (Calling) Yes?

JENNY. (Entering) It's the Maister o Allander, mem, and his Italian freind.

LUCY. Back already! Show them in, Jenny. (To KILMARDINNY) Now that's strange, uncle Tom.

KILMARDINNY. What's strange aboot it?

LUCY. They were going to be away for a fortnight at least. (As SIMON and BAROCCI are ushered in) Simon, you're back very suddenly. Has something gone wrong?

SIMON. Yes. Good afternoon, Lord Kilmardinny.

KILMARDINNY. Efternune.

LUCY. Signor Barocci, have you met my uncle?

KILMARDINNY. Ay ay, Signor Barocci and I are auld freinds. I peyed twa veesits to his exhibition, whan it opened in Edinburgh, and wad hae gane back again gin yer freind Dr Skinner hadna gotten to wark on it. Dinna tell me he followed ye to Perth, Signor.

SIGNOR. Si, yes, and to Dundee.

KILMARDINNY. Dundee! What connections has he there?

SIMON. None, except with his Church. Everywhere we went we found he had called a meeting of the local presbytery and given them his views on the exhibition, and they went back to their pulpits, with hardly an exception, and preached inflammatory sermons. The mobs he gathered both at Perth and Dundee had to be seen to be believed.

KILMARDINNY. It's a woner ye gat aff wi sae little skaith. Dae ye still hae the picturs?

SIMON. Yes. I had the help of my father's baron bailie at Perth, for we were lodging on Allander land, and we went to Dundee by boat, knowing we could stay aboard until we had found safe quarters and were assured of a good reception.

LUCY. That was clever.

SIMON. Not clever enough.

KILMARDINNY. Skinner had been there afore ye?

SIMON. Not only there, but somehow he had found that we were coming by boat, and even which boat.

KILMARDINNY. Sae there was a rabble waiting for ye at the harbour?

SIMON. Exactly. A howling horde of lunatic savages. We didn't dare risk even going alongside. We had to put to sea and land on the south coast of the firth about a mile from Broughty Ferry. We didn't dare make for the Ferry itself, in case there was another rabble there. There was a gale blowing up when we turned, and we ran into a storm. The mast was broken. It really is a miracle that we're here safe and sound, pictures and all, instead of at the bottom of the sea.

LUCY. Dear me, Dr Skinner has a lot to answer for.

KILMARDINNY. It isna juist Skinner's wark, Lucy. Nae ae man could steer up aa that bother gin the folk roun aboot him werena as bad as himsell.

SIGNOR. That is what I say, my lord. Simon keeps saying that it will be safe to hold the exhibition here in Edinburgh again because before very long it will be said in court that he has been lying with another man's wife, but he is not the only man in Scotland who says my pictures are filthy when they are told that the naked body is shown.

LUCY. (Excitedly) What did you say? Dr Skinner lying with another man's wife? What does he mean, Simon?

SIMON. It shouldn't perhaps have been mentioned yet, but it will no doubt soon be an open secret. Have you heard, my lord, that Sir Colin Kilgallon is filing suit for divorce?

LUCY. Sir Colin Kilgallon! But surely Dr Skinner hasn't been to bed with Lady Kilgallon! His own son's mother-in law! Isn't that incest, or something equally dreadful?

KILMARDINNY. Na, lassie, it's no even within the prohibited degrees o consanguinity. The law's gey queer, in some weys. But wha says the Doctor's been sleeping wi Leddy Kilgallon, or that Sir Colin's gaun to file suit for divorce?

SIMON. (Cagily) We first heard rumours in Perth.

KILMARDINNY. Rumours! Hhh!

SIMON. (Piqued into going too far) Ah yes, just as we thought. But they are in fact true.

KILMARDINNY. Na!

SIMON. Oh yes. My partner tells me that we have been asked to handle the business. He had been instructed before I returned. Sir Colin must be really badly roused. (Apologetically to LORD KILMARDINNY) This is all between ourselves, of course, my lord. Signor Barocci I told because he had already heard the rumours, and I'm sure Mrs. Lindsay will say nothing to anyone, at least until the case is proclaimed.

KILMARDINNY. (With professional disapproval) I hope no. It wad be a serious maitter for you, my lad, if Sir Colin kent ye were clashin aboot his private affairs.

SIMON. I am aware of that, my lord. I was careless. But it would have been a really serious slip only if Sir Colin had been concerned to keep his wife's infidelity secret. It seems he is determined to make it public.

KILMARDINNY. It'll mebbe prove to be a serious slip if Sir Colin daesna manage to prove his case. Leddy Kilgallon'll be efter ye for blackenin her character.

SIMON. I understand that, my lord.

LUCY. But when did it happen, Lady Kilgallon's infidelity?

KILMARDINNY. Nou cannie, Lucy. Ye suldna encourage a lawyer to gossip aboot his client's affairs.

LUCY. But he said he heard rumours in Perth. He can surely tell me about the rumours.

KILMARDINNY. Let him tell ye whan I'm no here, then. I'll mebbe hae the case to try. I'd better no allou mysell to be prejudiced. Guid efternune, Lucy.

LUCY. Good afternoon, uncle Tom, and thank you for everything.

(She holds up her cheek, very demurely, for him to kiss)

KILMARDINNY. (Having kissed her sedately) Behave yersell, nou. Guid efternune, Simon. Dinna encourage her.

SIMON. No, my lord. Good afternoon.

KILMARDINNY. Guid efternune, Signor Barocci. I hope
ye will be able to haud yer exhibition again. It was daen
us a service. We need faur mair opportunities here to
growe acquant wi warks o art. It's haurdly to be wonert
at that some o us are whiles a wee thing suspeecious o
them, when we see sae little o them frae ae year's end
til anither.

LUCY. Uncle Tom, I can see that if Sir Colin's case does
come to you for trial, you're going to find it very
difficult indeed to be impartial.

KILMARDINNY. I think, in case it daes, I'd better win awa
oot o here, and bide awa, mebbe, till it aa blaws ower.
Guid efternune, Signor.

SIGNOR. Good afternoon, my lord, and thank you.

KILMARDINNY. Thank you.

(He leaves)

LUCY. Now, Simon, what's this about Dr Skinner and Lady
Kilgallon?

SIMON. All I know definitely is that Sir Colin is filing suit
for divorce, and that my partner and I are to act for
him.

LUCY. Yes yes, but what about the rumours you heard in
Perth?

SIMON. They may not be true.

LUCY. There seems to be something behind them, at
least. Please don't tease me, Simon. Tell me what
you heard. If you don't I'll ask Signor Barocci.

SIGNOR. I do not know, except that he lay with another
man's wife.

88

SIMON. We heard the rumour first from the innkeeper at Perth. Sir Colin's groom told him that a servant girl had seen Lady Kilgallon coming out of Dr Skinner's room, and couldn't keep the news to herself.

LUCY. She told Sir Colin!

SIMON. No. She told the groom, and he told Sir Colin. He had some sort of grudge against Lady Kilgallon, apparently.

LUCY. And Sir Colin was furious?

SIMON. He sent for his factor, and told his factor to call his lawyers, and they have asked us to prepare case for counsel.

LUCY. You know, I'm not surprised.

SIMON. At Sir Colin?

LUCY. No, at Dr Skinner.

SIMON. I must say I was rather surprised at them both, though I didn't take long to remember that there had been rumours about Dr. Skinner. And perhaps it could have been expected of Lady Kilgallon too.

LUCY. I don't know her. Is she attractive?

SIMON. Not to me.

LUCY. But to men?

SIMON. I am a man, Lucy. Are you suggesting I am deficient in some way?

LUCY. Oh no, Simon. Of course not. But I mean to the sort of man Dr Skinner is?

SIMON. I don't quite follow. What sort of man is Dr. Skinner, in the sense under discussion?

LUCY. Well, more interested in the possibility of

physical conquest than in the development of a personal relationship, if I may put it that way.

SIMON. I think you put it admirably. But is he really like that? I knew he liked to exercise his fascination, but always for purposes of material advantage.

LUCY. Oh no, he sometimes exercises his fascination where there is no hope of material advantage whatsoever.

SIMON. Lucy! He hasn't been exercising his fascination on you?

LUCY. Oh but yes. Do you remember the last time you called here, just before you set off for Perth?

SIMON. Yes. Yes, I remember! He was here when we arrived.

LUCY. Don't you remember how unpleasant he was?

SIMON. I certainly do.

LUCY. You had interrupted him. He had just declared a guilty passion, which he couldn't control.

SIMON. Good God, really! What a scoundrel! And he goes straight to Perth and does the same again with his own son's mother-in-law!

LUCY. More successfully than with me, evidently.

SIMON. Lucy, did he lay a finger on you?

LUCY. Oh no.

SIMON. If he did, I will call him out.

LUCY. Simon, you mustn't think of any such thing. You mustn't indicate in any way that I've breathed a word of what happened.

SIMON. The very declaration itself was an insult. He should be called out. What do you do in Italy, Barocci, when a man insults a defenceless woman by pressing his attentions on her?

SIGNOR. Swords or pistols.

SIMON. You see. I'll have to call him out. It's a matter of honour.

SIGNOR. You cannot, because of his black cloth. We do not challenge priests.

SIMON. You're right. I had forgotten. Then what do you do with them?

SIGNOR. Pay a servant to slit his throat.

LUCY. Signor Barocci! You mustn't put ideas into Simon's head.

SIGNOR. Forgive me. I am a stranger here.

LUCY. Simon, you must forget what I have told you. He didn't really annoy me. He was rather pathetic, really.

SIMON. The man's a scoundrel. He was obviously acting a part. Trying to seduce you.

LUCY. Oh Simon!

SIMON. Obviously.

LUCY. Well, don't be so heated about it. It's all over now and he isn't likely to try it again. He'll be disgraced, won't he, when Sir Colin's case is brought into court.

SIMON. Completely exposed and very deservedly ruined, I should think.

LUCY. Then I agree with you, Simon, that he isn't likely to try to stir up trouble now, if Signor Barocci holds another exhibition.

SIMON. That's what I tell him, but he won't listen.

SIGNOR. You heard what my lord your uncle said, that Dr
Skinner could not have stirred up trouble if most of the
people here had not been exactly like himself.

SIMON. Yes, Giorgio, but you forget that just as he was
leaving, Lord Kilmardinny also said that he hoped you
would hold an exhibition.

LUCY. Yes, which was as much as to say that he hoped Dr
Skinner would be disgraced, and that if he was you could
hold your exhibition again without fear of opposition.

SIMON. It's true, Giorgio. I'm quite sure that without Dr
Skinner to stir up trouble you have nothing to fear.

SIGNOR. Simon, I am sorry, but I cannot forget my landlord, Mr Davidson. His face, when he told me that he
had been forbidden to let me exhibit my pictures. When
he was told that his minister would rebuke him from
the preaching box. And that he would be excommunicated.
Excommunicated!

SIMON. But you can exhibit your pictures now in some
house in another parish, and nothing will happen.

SIGNOR. No, Simon. I cannot forget the rabble on the
bridge at Perth, crying filthy, and sacrilege, and
idolatry, and burn them at the cross, and send him
forth, out of the town, on a stang. That is a wooden
horse, Mrs. Lindsay. They threatened to carry me
out of the town with one leg on each side of a tree.

LUCY. But that was Perth, Signor Barocci.

SIGNOR. Si, that was Perth, yes. But Dundee. It was
worse. The rabble on the harbour wall. Drown him,
they cried. Sink the boat and all that is in it. And then
the storm. And the boat creaking. And the mast
breaking. And the waves, like mountains. Worse than
on the French channel. No, I am sorry. I return to
England. The people there are more tolerant.

LUCY. Oh, Signor Barocci, you shouldn't judge the Scots
as a whole by the behaviour of an ignorant rabble in

two insignificant provincial towns.

SIGNOR. All the trouble started here, in Edinburgh.

LUCY. Yes, with just one man. But he will be disgraced, and your exhibition will be safe.

SIMON. She's right, you know, Giorgio. You ought to stay.

LUCY. He hasn't arranged to leave, has he?

SIMON. Yes, in spite of all that I could do to prevent it.

SIGNOR. I am sorry, Mrs. Lindsay, to seem ungrateful. Some of you have been very kind. Simon, my dear friend has ensured that I have suffered no loss. But I would lie if I did not admit that I am terrified. I have lost my courage. And I love my pictures. I cannot stay.

SIMON. I really think it's tragic, Giorgio, that you should decide to leave just when we have Skinner beaten.

SIGNOR. I am sorry, my friends, but I have made my arrangements, and sail from Leith tomorrow.

LUCY. Tomorrow!

SIGNOR. Yes, and I pray that there will be no rabble at the harbour to stop me.

SIMON. How can there possibly be, if you haven't advertised your departure.

SIGNOR. I have not advertised it.

LUCY. I'm sorry, Signor Barocci, that you're leaving like this.

SIGNOR. I am sorry too.

LUCY. I feel so ashamed for my country.

SIMON. Oh come, Lucy. He hasn't really given our country a chance. We're not all bigoted fanatics and hypocrites.

SIGNOR. That is true. I have said before. Some of you have been very kind.

SIMON. But the majority of us have treated you badly. Yes, Barocci, I suppose you are right, and I can only apologise for ever having thought of asking you to come here.

SIGNOR. You meant well, Simon.

SIMON. Yes.

LUCY. Would you like some tea? I can ask Jenny to serve it now.

SIMON. It's very kind of you, Lucy, but I really must see my partner and hear about the Kilgallon case.

LUCY. Oh yes.

SIGNOR. And I must prepare for my voyage to London.

LUCY. London?

SIGNOR. Yes. Good-bye, Mrs. Lindsay, and thank you for being so sympathetic, and your uncle, for being so appreciative.

LUCY. Good-bye, Signor Barocci. I feel so sorry.

SIGNOR. Yes.

SIMON. Good-bye, then, Lucy. I shall see you soon again, I hope.

LUCY. I hope so. Good-bye.

(She ushers them out, closes the door, stands for a little, then moves to the window and looks out. Suddenly there is a knock, and the door opens)

JENNY. Dr. Skinner, mem!

LUCY. Dr. Skinner!

JENNY. (Whispering hurriedly) He cam afore, but whan I telt him wha was wi ye he said he wad caa back!

LUCY. (As DR. SKINNER appears) Very well, Jenny. I'm not at home until Dr. Skinner leaves.

JENNY. Na, mem.

(She leaves and closes the door)

LUCY. (Coldly) Good afternoon, Doctor.

SKINNER. Good afternoon. The Master of Allander has just been here, with that Italian.

LUCY. They are friends of mine.

SKINNER. I waited for them to leave.

LUCY. That was very wise of you, Doctor.

SKINNER. I see from your manner that they have said something to prejudice you against me.

LUCY. You've taken great pains to prevent Signor Barocci from holding his exhibition.

SKINNER. I did what I saw to be my clear Christian duty.

LUCY. Signor Barocci is a Christian too, Doctor.

SKINNER. A Papist.

LUCY. That hardly affects the artistic value of his pictures.

SKINNER. It affects what he regards as suitable subject matter.

LUCY. What could be more suitable than the great stories from scripture, or from the classical mythologies?

95

SKINNER. Our religion forbids us to portray the Lord, and decency forbids us to display the naked body.

LUCY. We have argued this question before, Doctor. I have no desire to go over the ground again.

SKINNER. They have obviously said something to prejudice you against me.

LUCY. I am angry with you for reviling a really wonderful exhibition of beautiful and moving pictures, and stirring up hatred against a distinguished visitor to our country, and endangering his life.

SKINNER. Nonsense. He would never have been in danger if he had respected our standards. It's the least a visitor can do.

LUCY. You have made me ashamed of my countrymen. You're so fanatical, and bigoted, and prurient.

SKINNER. Prurient!

LUCY. Yes, prurient. What else does your pretended fear of the human body amount to?

SKINNER. Pretended fear!

LUCY. Yes.

SKINNER. I see. I knew they had been saying something.

LUCY. Saying what?

SKINNER. Spreading vile rumours to discredit me, because I have frustrated them.

LUCY. Rumours? What sort of Rumours?

SKINNER. Filthy lies.

LUCY. What sort of lies?

SKINNER. They have had the nerve to say that I have

committed adultery with the mother of my son's wife.

LUCY. Is it not true?

SKINNER. True! My dear Mrs. Lindsay, can you really believe for a minute that I could be so base: so unnatural!

LUCY. I think you <u>could</u> be so base, Dr. Skinner.

SKINNER. You think I could!

LUCY. Have you forgotten your last visit?

SKINNER. I see. So you misjudged me, and thought perhaps that I was leading up to an improper suggestion? My dear Mrs. Lindsay, you have been quite mistaken. You knew little of me not to realise that my feelings were genuine, although it was perhaps wrong of me to declare them, in view of your married state. Yet I made it clear at the time, I think, that I did so under an irresistible compulsion, and that my intentions towards you were honourable, and would be proved so if you were ever in a position to obtain a divorce.

LUCY. Did you say just the same sort of thing to Lady Kilgallon?

SKINNER. Mrs. Lindsay, you are being deliberately offensive. You have obviously been poisoned against me. You believe their vile story.

LUCY. It seems a very probable one.

SKINNER. You would hardly be so sure unless they had told their story with some appearance of having irrefutable evidence. What exactly did they say to substantiate it?

LUCY. (Hedging) Nothing. I just think, knowing you, that it seems a very probable one.

SKINNER. I should have thought that, knowing me, you would have laughed at their lies.

LUCY. On the contrary. I judged that with a woman of easy virtue the tactics you used with me would prove very successful.

SKINNER. I would hardly have called Lady Kilgallon a woman of easy virtue.

LUCY. She must have been, to allow you to succeed.

SKINNER. You wrong her as well as me by believing your friends' lies.

LUCY. My friends are truthful men, Doctor.

SKINNER. But I am not!

LUCY. I no longer think you so.

SKINNER. (Trying again) You think you know something. Tell me why you are so convinced that their story is true.

LUCY. (Hedging again) Because it fits your behaviour towards me.

SKINNER. I tell you that is not so. My behaviour towards you was the result of a sudden breaking down in a resolve that I have kept honourably for months in the face of constant temptation; a resolve to conceal my genuine love for you until you were free, and I could declare it honourably. I know it was wrong of me to be so weak, and perhaps knowing the strain I was under in pretending mere friendship I should have kept away from you, but I had to see you. I couldn't live without seeing you. I love you.

LUCY. You have lived without seeing me for well over a week. Was the strain so overwhelming that you had to have Lady Kilgallon to console you?

SKINNER. (Trying a new line) Lady Kilgallon again. Why do you harp on her? Are you jealous?

LUCY. (Indignantly) Jealous, Dr. Skinner! Jealous!

98

SKINNER. I mean, did the silly story they told you perhaps make you feel angry because you thought I had been false to you?

LUCY. I certainly did think you had been false to what you declared your feelings to be. And it did make me angry with you, yes.

SKINNER. But then, you see, you had believed the story. Lucy, there is no need for you to be angry. It was a lie.

LUCY. (Leading him on) You swear it?

SKINNER. I give you my solemn oath.

LUCY. And you really declare that you love me, and that if I was ever able to obtain a divorce you would ask me to be your wife?

SKINNER. (Blandly) Yes.

LUCY. My uncle Lord Kilmardinny was here today. He says that my lawyers in Jamaica will be able to procure sworn testimony that my husband is living with another woman, by whom he has two children. Divorce now is only a matter of time. (As SKINNER pales) Well, aren't you pleased?

SKINNER. Eh, yes, delighted.

LUCY. Doctor, you are a bare-faced liar. You have turned as white as a sheet.

SKINNER. It's just that it's so sudden. The culmination of months, of years, of hoping against hope.

LUCY. Years! That's interesting. How many? Have you really been in love with me for years?

SKINNER. Since I first set eyes on you.

LUCY. Your second wife was still alive then.

SKINNER. I mean, since shortly after I lost her.

LUCY. Don't try to keep it up, Doctor. I am not impressed.

SKINNER. You do know something.

LUCY. (Unable to hold out) Yes, I know something.

SKINNER. Tell me: what are they saying? What are they saying to make you so sure that they aren't lying?

LUCY. (Carefully) There is a rumour, Doctor, that Sir Colin Kilgallon is going to petition for divorce, with you as co-respondent.

SKINNER. How did you hear this? From your uncle?

LUCY. My uncle never discusses his judicial business with me, Doctor.

SKINNER. From the Master of Allander.

LUCY. Signor Barocci heard the rumour in Perth.

SKINNER. And you believed a rumour picked up in Perth?

LUCY. It came from a source very close to Sir Colin.

SKINNER. From whom?

LUCY. I am not going to tell you, Doctor.

SKINNER. Who told Sir Colin that I lay with his wife? That is what I want to know. Whoever he is, he's a liar, and I will bring his lie home to him. Who was it?

LUCY. You will no doubt learn when he appears in court as a witness.

SKINNER. There is to be a case, then. It is more than a mere rumour.

LUCY. I haven't said so.

SKINNER. You talked about this man appearing in court.

LUCY. He will, won't he, if the rumour is true.

SKINNER. And you refuse to name him?

LUCY. It would be unwise.

SKINNER. (Cunningly) Tell me, when does your own case come up?

LUCY. My own case?

SKINNER. For your divorce.

LUCY. Not until I instruct my lawyers to go ahead with it.

SKINNER. It will not precede mine, then?

LUCY. (Not understanding) Oh no.

SKINNER. Sir Colin <u>has</u> issued instructions, then?

LUCY. Has he?

SKINNER. You implied it.

LUCY. You are very clever, Doctor, but I wonder if in the end you will turn out to have been quite clever enough.

SKINNER. You think I am ruined. Don't you?

LUCY. It looks like it.

SKINNER. And you have no pity?

LUCY. Oh yes, pity. But I see justice in it.

SKINNER. You are gloating. You, a woman who pretended friendship. You did more. You led me on, provoking me with suggestive movements of your body, and titillating me with salacious conversation. You deliberately set out to trap me into a declaration of passion, so that you could gloat over my guilt.

LUCY. Rubbish.

SKINNER. Because I am a minister of the gospel; because I held the Lord in awe and would not admit his likeness in the work of human hands; because it was my duty to denounce the wanton exposure of the human body, to the end that jaded men might stimulate their faded appetites, to the neglect and perdition of their immortal souls; because, I say, of every Christian duty laid upon me by my cloth, you deliberately took advantage of my widowed condition, and my unsatisfied flesh, to bring about my ruin.

LUCY. Dr. Skinner, I think you're going mad. It was Lady Kilgallon who took advantage of your unsatisfied flesh, if it wasn't rather the other way about; and if anyone but yourself has ruined you, it was she, not I.

SKINNER. So you think I'm ruined? And no doubt young Adair and that Italian think I'm ruined. And Sir Colin Kilgallon. And your uncle, the generous patron of the arts. You'll all have to think again, my dear. There will be no scandal. No one is going to ruin the Reverend Samuel Skinner. There's too much at stake.

(He leaves abruptly as LUCY stares in bewilderment.)

ACT FIVE

(DR. SKINNER's study in the Tolbooth manse,
Edinburgh.
DR. SKINNER is discovered sitting at his desk, staring
before him, his hands clutching some legal documents.
SAUNDERS WATSON enters to him.)

SAUNDERS. Ye sent for me, Doctor. Is there something
wrang?

SKINNER. There is, Saunders, and I need your help. Sit
down, will you?

SAUNDERS. Thank ye, Doctor.

SKINNER. As ruling elder in the Tolbooth you will no doubt
have its welfare very much at heart?

SAUNDERS. Oh ay, Doctor.

SKINNER. And you'll be aware how much its welfare
depends on my reputation?

SAUNDERS. Oh ay, Doctor. The weilfare o ony kirk
depends on its meenister's reputation, and that's
what's gart the Tolbooth flourish abune aa ithers.

SKINNERS. It's kind of you to say so, Saunders.

SAUNDERS. Hoots na, Doctor, it's juist the truith.
There's nae mair upricht man nor better preacher in
the country. Dod, but ye dang that Italian doun, that
micht hae tried to haud anither exhibition o thae
Papish picturs. They say he's sailed frae Leith, and

we hae seen the last o him.

SKINNER. Yes, Saunders, but my work for the Lord has made me enemies.

SAUNDERS. Ye can aye coont on that, Doctor.

SKINNER. Yes, but it sometimes looks as if one's enemies may prevail. I have been struck a sore blow, Saunders.

SAUNDERS. I'm wae to hear it, Doctor.

SKINNER. I have been given notice that I am to be accused in the divorce court of committing adultery.

SAUNDERS. Adultery! You! Wha has the nerve to say the like o that?

SKINNER. You will be astonished, Saunders. It's alleged by none other than my own son's father-in-law, Sir Colin Kilgallon.

SAUNDERS. Sir Colin! I thocht he had been stricken dumb, Doctor.

SKINNER. He had, but some foul liar, in league with the young Master of Allander, told him that I had spent a night with his lady, and the shock so affected him that he recovered his speech, and used it to initiate divorce proceedings.

SAUNDERS. Someane in league wi the young Maister o Allander?

SKINNER. Yes.

SAUNDERS. The man that brocht that Italian ower frae Rome?

SKINNER. Yes.

SAUNDERS. Naebody'll believe the like o him against the like o you, Doctor.

104

SKINNER. I'm afraid you're mistaken, Saunders. There are quite a number in the town who call themselves patrons of the arts, who profess regret that the Italian has gone, and some of them are regrettably men of position and influence. Quite a number are members of the legal fraternity.

SAUNDERS. Dae I no ken it. The Music Society's nearly aa lawyers thegither.

SKINNER. Some of them even judges, Saunders.

SAUNDERS. Oh ay, Doctor. Kilmardinny for ane.

SKINNER. Exactly. And it seems quite possible that if this divorce case goes ahead, Lord Kilmardinny may be the officiating judge.

SAUNDERS. That wad doun the scales a wee against ye, Doctor, for he had a essay on the Italian's exhibition in the Idler, praisin it, and miscaain his ain kith and kin for wantin to hoond the dirty blaggard awa oot o here and ower the Border.

SKINNER. I read it.

SAUNDERS. Ay, Doctor, but I wadna let it fash ye. The feck o folk think the wey we dae.

SKINNER. But it may be Lord Kilmardinny who officiates at this divorce case.

SAUNDERS. Ay, Doctor, but nae judge can gang against the evidence, and if ye hae a guid coonsel, Doctor, he'll sune expose ony witness that daurs to tell a lee aboot ye.

SKINNER. That's a very comforting theory, Saunders, but things don't always turn out that way. Suppose an evil man with power over an infatuated girl, who compels her to swear to a lie, then you have two people prepared to swear to the lie, and it becomes acceptable as evidence.

105

SAUNDERS. But if it a lee, Doctor, ye suld be able to fin
twa witnesses or mair to nail it doun.

SKINNER. Not so, Saunders. Take the present case. Sir
Colin's groom has a spite at his mistress, for some
injustice she is alleged to have inflicted on him, and
he's succeeded in persuading one of the chamber-maids
to swear that she saw her coming out of my bedroom,
one morning before dawn, when I was last at Auchengool
as a guest.

SAUNDERS. The chalmer-maid saw Leedy Kilgallon?

SKINNER. No, but she is ready to swear she did. And I
can produce no witness to prove that at the moment
Lady Kilgallon was alleged to be leaving my room, she
was in fact elsewhere.

SAUNDERS. Mebbe no, Doctor, but shairly ye can fin
evidence o the spite the groo has at Leddy Kilgallon?

SKINNER. Possibly, but...

SAUNDERS. Oh ay, Doctor. And ye said, I think, that this
groom had some pouer ower the chalmer-maid. Nae
dout he had haen his will o her, and she was feart he
wad forsake her. Shairly ye can fin witnesses to prove
onything o that kind?

SKINNER. I don't feel confident, Saunders. Although I
have no doubt that what I have told you is true, in
court it would be treated as hearsay.

SAUNDERS. But if ye were to get the lawyers on the job,
Doctor, they'd sune fin the evidence ye want. The
truith can aye be fund, Doctor, gin ye persevere in
the sairch.

SKINNER. I doubt it very much, Saunders, and in any
case I think the disastrous effect of the mere fact of
the case coming into court at all would be sufficient
reason for taking whatever steps we can to stop it.

SAUNDERS. Stop it!

106

SKINNER. Yes, Saunders, stop it. If this case comes
before the court there will be a great deal of mud
thrown, and no matter how innocent I am proved to be,
some of it will stick. And we have to think not only of
myself, but of the church of which I am a minister. Its
standing will suffer if my reputation is tainted.

SAUNDERS. But naebody bune a haundfou o the maist
extreme Moderates wad believe a word against yer
character, Doctor. Yer record is weill kent: minister
o the Tolbooth; ex-moderator o the presbytery o Perth;
secretary o the Society for the Propagation o Christian
knowledge. Naebody in his senses wad believe ye could
commit ony sin at aa, Doctor, faur less adultery.

SKINNER. I am touched by your faith in me, Saunders, but
I am convinced that if this case comes into court some
mud will stick. And since I have the good of my church,
and of the Church of Scotland, and of the Christian
cause itself, very much at heart, I am determined to
go to any length to stop it.

SAUNDERS. But hou can ye stop it, Doctor? Ye're no gaun
to settle wi Sir Colin oot o coort: pey him siller to hush
the haill thing up?

SKINNER. He might not agree to such a course, even if I
could bring myself to admit to a sin I had not committed.

SAUNDERS. Na. Then hou are ye gaun to stop the case,
Doctor?

SKINNER. What I am going to propose may astonish you,
Saunders.

SAUNDERS. Eh?

SKINNER. Don't condemn it without very careful consider-
ation. At first it may startle you, but give yourself
time to recover from your first shock, and you will
find it not such a preposterous idea.

SAUNDERS. What, Doctor?

SKINNER. I sent for you, Saunders, not just because you are my ruling elder, but because you are an undertaker.

SAUNDERS. (Understanding) Doctor!

SKINNER. Do you understand?

SAUNDERS. Ye arena thinkin o haein yersell buried, mebbe, while ye slip aff abroad?

SKINNER. It's the only way to save the good name of the church, Saunders.

SAUNDERS. But ye wad hae to practise deceit, Doctor; on yer congregation; on yer relatives and freinds; on yer very ain son himsell. Yer daith wad cause them grief, Doctor. And ye wad involve ither folk in deceit tae. Ye wad hae to fin some medical man to sweir that he had attended ye and that ye were badly wi some fatal disease or ither. What explanation were ye thinkin could be gien for yer daith, Doctor?

SKINNER. I was hoping that you and some medical friend could say that I had been stricken by a palsy.

SAUNDERS. There ye are, ye see. Ye wad hae to ask twa o us to lee, forbye leein yersell, for ye wad hae to pretend to be someane else, and tak a fause name.

SKINNER. Yes I know, Saunders, and yet, for the sake of the kirk, we should be able to shoulder the burden of one comparatively minor sin. And we can be comforted in the anguish of our repentance by God's assurance of forgiveness in the end.

SAUNDERS. Ay, Doctor, but there's the maitter o my honour as an undertaker. It's a responsible tred, for it's open to serious abuses. Ye micht be wantin to bury the corp o someane ye had murdert, Doctor.

SKINNER. Me! Murder someone!

SAUNDERS. It's juist an instance o the kind o thing that micht growe to be a habit if folk in my tred werena to

108

be trustit, Doctor.

SKINNER. But it has no relevance to this scheme of mine, Saunders, where I am asking you simply to allow me to disappear in order to prevent the good name of the church from being tainted by the mere fact of the appearance of its minister in the divorce court. Surely you don't refuse to help me to protect the good name of the church, Saunders.

SAUNDERS. I dinna like the deceit involved. I'm sorry to seem to be preachin at ye, Doctor, but ye'll see for yersell that if we were to try to gang through wi this plan we wad hae to lee like heathens.

SKINNER. The whole affair would blow over in a few weeks.

SAUNDERS. Ye dae yersell in injustice, Doctor. Ye dinna ken hou weill ye're thocht o. There wad hae to be a memorial. There wad be an appeal, and syne some conseederation o the form it wad tak, then the orderin o the wark, whateir it was to be, and syne the service o dedication. The haill maitter micht hang on for weill ower a year, and aa that time yer relatives and freinds bein remindit o their loss, and the like o mysell, that was in the secret, remindit o my lee. Na na, Doctor, it winna dae. Ye'll hae to show mair faith in yersell, and in the pouer o the truith to prevail, and bid here and fetch the case.

SKINNER. I'm disappointed in you, Saunders.

SAUNDERS. (Beginning to grow impatient) Disappeintit, Doctor, whan aa I'm daein is to try to keep you yersell to the rules o strict Christian behaviour. Ye suld be pleased that yer teachin has borne sich fruit, Doctor, that ye canna coax me to tell a lee for aa yer gift o the gab. Nou pou yersell thegither, Doctor. I kne it'll be an ordeal to hae to face a lot o leears in coort, but ye're weill thocht o, and yer faes arena, and wi guid lawyers ye'll win through withoot skaith.

SKINNER. Then you refuse to help me?

SAUNDERS. I dinna think ye're juist yersell, Doctor, or ye wadna be askin me.

SKINNER. You compel me to humble myself, Saunders.

SAUNDERS. (Not understanding) Na na, Doctor, juist to pou yersell thegither.

SKINNER. You don't understand. (Pause) I'm a guilty man, Saunders. A poor sinner. I did commit adultery with Lady Kilgallon.

SAUNDERS. (After a pause) I see.

SKINNER. A wanton woman, Saunders. I was too weak to withstand her.

SAUNDERS. But this'll ruin ye.

SKINNER. Not only me, Saunders, and that doesn't matter. It'll bring disgrace and ridicule on the Tolbooth church and on the Church of Scotland itself, and on the Christian religion. It must be kept from becoming public knowledge. Don't you see that?

SAUNDERS. Ay, Doctor.

SKINNER. Then you'll do as I ask?

SAUNDERS. There's the medical side o the maitter, Doctor.

SKINNER. Tom Forrest the surgeon will help me, for he has come to me before in troubles of his own, and I have obliged him with the strictest secrecy. If he is willing to swear to the fact of my death, and its physical cause, will you have any difficulty?

SAUNDERS. Some awkwardness, mebbe, wi my man on the job, and wi Girzie Dodds yer hoose-keeper. But I daursay I'll win bye.

SKINNER. Then there's no time to waste. Find Tom Forrest for me quickly. The sooner I see him the

110

better. He'll be in the Sheep's Head Tavern about this time, I should think. Don't tell him what I want till I have sounded him out, but fetch him as quickly as you can.

SAUNDERS. Ay, Doctor. (Turning at the door) Oh, ye micht stert cairryin on an airmfou o books, Doctor, ilka time ye're oot, and hidin them whaur Girzie winna see them. If I took ony aff the shelves here she micht smell a rat.

SKINNER. I see. Yes, I'll attend to that. And you be ready to act within a few days.

SAUNDERS. Fin the books sune, then.

SKINNER. Yes. (Knock) Yes?

(The door opens and JOSEPH SKINNER enters, breathless and excited)

JOSEPH. Oh, you have someone here.

SKINNER. Joseph! I had no idea you were in town. Good afternoon then, Saunders. You know what I want.

SAUNDERS. Ay, Doctor. Guid efternune, Mr. Joseph.

JOSEPH. Good afternoon, Saunders.

(SAUNDERS leaves, closing the door quietly)

SKINNER. Has something happened?

JOSEPH. Father, prepare yourself for a shock.

SKINNER. What is it?

JOSEPH. Kitty's father had another stroke last night. He passed away this morning.

SKINNER. (Quietly) Sir Colin! Dead!

JOSEPH. Yes.

SKINNER. It is the hand of God. Shielding his own. I know I am unworthy but I am His instrument, and therefore He has saved me. (Pause) There will be no divorce case.

JOSEPH. No.

SKINNER. My enemies may spread filthy talk about it, but nothing will ever be proved in court.

JOSEPH. No.

SKINNER. I shall be able to remain and carry on with my work.

JOSEPH. Were you planning to go away?

SKINNER. I thought it might be wiser.

JOSEPH. I don't know why you don't retire anyway, father. You have sufficient of a fortune to live like a gentleman.

SKINNER. It is my work, Joseph. I revel in it.

JOSEPH. But there will be some talk, father, even with the divorce case dropped.

SKINNER. It will not be believed if I remain at my post, Joseph.

JOSEPH. (Conceding) Perhaps it is less likely to be.

SKINNER. I have no doubt of it whatsoever. And if you have any tendency to think I may be uncomfortable because of any incompatibility between my duty and my recent behaviour, remember that in this instance I sinned for your sake. You know that.

JOSEPH. Yes, father.

SKINNER. Sir Colin's estate is entailed on Kitty?

JOSEPH. Yes, but it is heavily burdened with debt.

SKINNER. Will her mother clear it?

JOSEPH. She may.

SKINNER. How has she taken Sir Colin's death?

JOSEPH. She pays the usual homage of tears and a long face, but I am sure she is glad to be free of all the worry he gave her.

SKINNER. Has she seen anything at all of the Earl of Allander lately, or said anything to indicate that she is still interested?

JOSEPH. The Earl did call to pay his respect just before I left. I thought he came rather quickly. Rather more quickly than was seemly.

SKINNER. But has Lady Kilgallon said anything to indicate whether or not she returns his interest?

JOSEPH. I can't say she tries to repel him, but she is slightly less effusive than before your, eh, last visit.

SKINNER. We must keep her out of his clutches at all costs. It would be a tragedy if your prospects were ruined because the need for male companionship compelled her to accept his advances.

JOSEPH. What troubles me is that she is keen on title. That was why she married Sir Colin.

SKINNER. An earl would be a step higher.

JOSEPH. Yes.

SKINNER. But the man is almost emaciated.

JOSEPH. Yes.

SKINNER. She is still vigorous. He would never content her.

JOSEPH. No.

SKINNER. We must ensure that he is never put to the test. How has Kitty taken her father's death?

JOSEPH. She's badly shocked. She was fond of him.

SKINNER. We must be careful to respect her sorrow.

JOSEPH. Yes, father. Sir Colin's death has lifted a great burden off our spirits, but it would be unseemly to let Kitty even sense it.

SKINNER. How did she view the charges brought against her mother and me?

JOSEPH. I don't think she really believed them. She said she didn't.

SKINNER. Will she come to believe them, do you think, if her mother and I should remain, eh, friends?

JOSEPH. I should be careful to let her know as little as possible, for some time at least.

SKINNER. I quite agree. How is her health? Is she still suffering from sickness?

JOSEPH. The sickness has almost gone. Now it's gluttony. She eats like a horse.

SKINNER. An excellent sign. After all, she is eating for two now. I only hope her grief over her father's death will not destroy her appetite.

JOSEPH. I daresay there is a danger, but her mother's determined to keep her from brooding. She is bringing her to Edinburgh to buy clothes.

SKINNER. Clothes! Oh, of course, mourning.

JOSEPH. Yes.

SKINNER. And when are they coming?

JOSEPH. They are here.

114

SKINNER. Here! Already!

JOSEPH. Yes. Her mother said the sooner she was distracted from her grief the better.

SKINNER. Did they come south with you?

JOSEPH. No, I rode ahead. But they turned up in Edinburgh before I left to come here to you.

SKINNER. Left?

JOSEPH. We are all to stay with Kitty's aunt, Lady Kilcogie. Her mother thought that to stay here might be inadvisable. But they will be calling soon.

SKINNER. Calling! I hope they won't be seen!

JOSEPH. Does it matter now?

SKINNER. Oh. Of course not. The more natural their behaviour now the better. You know, Joseph, I had suddenly forgotten the good news.

JOSEPH. Good news, father! You really will have to be more careful than that in front of Kitty. A single remark like that and she would learn everything.

SKINNER. You are quite right, my boy. I must be much more careful. Do I hear a stir?

(Murmuration)

JOSEPH. Yes. They are here, I think.

(There is a knock at the door and it is immediately opened by LADY KILGALLON, who enters and ushers in KITTY)

LADY K. Can we come in?

SKINNER. (Rising) My dear Lady Kilgallon, I have just heard the sad news. (To KITTY, taking her hands in his and speaking with an air of great distress) My

dear child, how I grieve for you. The loss of a father.
So important to a girl. So many memories. From early
childhood. The dearest of all. So poignant.

(She bursts into tears)

But loss comes to us all, my dear, and in your case you
have been given time to prepare yourself, and I know
you will be brave. There now, don't cry, my dear. You
still have Joseph. Look after her, Joseph.

JOSEPH. Yes, father. (Placing a chair for her) Come,
my dear. Sit.

(She sits, crying steadily and snuffling)

SKINNER. (To LADY KILGALLON) And you, my dear
lady. Your sorrow too must be well nigh unendurable.
A long and intimate companionship, even if it comes
gradually to a close, with early and constant warning
of its impending end, cannot be finally concluded
without grief too deep for words. Memories of youth
and courtship. Marriage. The birth of a child.
Precious events which can never be forgotten. All
crowd the mind and overwhelm it.

LADY K. (Playing up, perhaps, for the sake of KITTY) Ay,
Doctor. We had twenty cantie years afore he had his
first stroke.

SKINNER. They will be difficult to forget.

LADY K. Ay.

SKINNER. But the Lord in His wisdom has ordained that
what we find difficult to forget we like best to
remember. Beyond the present sorrow is always a
past joy.

LADY K. Ay. I woner if Joseph could tak Kitty into the
paurlor and let her lie back on the sofa. Thae chairs
o yours here are gey hard on the banes, Doctor, and
the lassie's haen a lang day's traivel.

116

JOSEPH. Certainly, mother.

LADY K. Ye'll realise, Kitty my dear, that nou yer puir
faither's passed awa there are a wheen maitters I hae
to discuss wi Joseph's faither aboot yer jeynt prospects.

KITTY. I'm shair o the estate onywey. My faither telt me
that.

LADY K. Ye're quite richt, my dear, and naebody's gaun
to try and tak it frae ye. Aa I'm concerned to dae is
let ye hae it free o debt, sae that ye can pass it on to
yer ain auldest wi yer mind easy.

JOSEPH. Yes, dear, let us go and leave them to talk
business.

SKINNER. That's right, Joseph. Look after her well.

LADY K. Hae a guid rest, my dear.

     (JOSEPH and KITTY leave)

SKINNER. (Awkwardly) I really do feel sorry for you in
your bereavement, Lady Kilgallon, although it would
be hypocritical in me not to acknowledge that it
removes a threat of ruin from both of us; or from me,
at least.

LADY K. Ye needna feel sorry for me, Doctor. I had lost
my man ower lang afore his daith for it to mak ony
difference.

SKINNER. You did have time to prepare your mind for his
passing, certainly.

LADY K. Ay, Doctor. Am I to tak it frae yer mainner that
ye regret what happened the last time we were
thegither?

SKINNER. (Anxious not to be too crude) My dear Phemie,
I have repented of it on my bended knees. I feel so
ashamed to have had so little self control that I could
profane your person, and force you into adultery, when

with a little patience I could have waited until I was able to offer myself honourably, and accept you without shame.

LADY K. Samuel, dae ye still want me? (As he hesitates) Or dae ye no?

SKINNER. Want you? Well, of course I find you attractive; far too attractive, in view of the weakness of my character, as you know.

LADY K. That means ye canna resist me, daes it?

SKINNER. I suppose it does, yes.

LADY K. I wish ye could aye say juist what ye mean, but bein a minister I suppose ye canna.

SKINNER. Well, I do have to make finer distinctions than most people.

LADY K. Nae dout. Nae dout. And it winna fash me gin I can juist be shair whaur I am wi ye. If ye canna resist me ye had better mairry me, for ye wadna feel very comfortable gin ye didna, aye haein to repent.

SKINNER. But the scandal.

LADY K. Oh I dinna mean juist at ance. We maun wait till efter a dacent interval.

SKINNER. It must be for some time, and even after a considerable interval there will still be some scandal, in view of our unusual relationship to each other, through Joseph and Kitty.

LADY K. I hae lookit it up in the Bible, Samuel. Leviticus eichteen. And I can fin naething against it.

SKINNER. You are right, there is nothing. 'The nakedness of thy father's wife's daughter, begotten of thy father, she is thy sister, thou shalt not uncover her nakedness.' Kitty would become Joseph's father's wife's daughter, but not begotten of his father.

LADY K. Juist what I said. There's naething against it.

SKINNER. People will talk, nevertheless.

LADY K. Gin there's naething wrang wi it there's naething wrang wi it, Samuel, sae let them clash.

SKINNER. I quite agree.

LADY K. Weill, that's settled, and I can tell ye it's a relief. And ye winna regret it. I'll no juist see that Kitty has Kilgallon free o debt. I'll help Joseph wi his new shed.

SKINNER. How kind of you.

LADY K. He has a guid heid on him. He minds me o my faither. He'll dae weill, will Joseph.

SKINNER. I'm glad you think so. I'm sure you're a good judge.

LADY K. Nane better. (Rising) Weill, Samuel, I'd better fin Kitty and tak her to caa on the dress-maker. There's little time awtween daith and the burial. I'll see ye whan ye come to Auchengool for it.

SKINNER. Yes. (Knock) Oh, I think this will be one of my elders on kirk business. (Calling) Yes?

(The door opens and SAUNDERS sticks his head in)

Come in and sit down, Saunders. I shan't keep you a minute. (To LADY KILGALLON, formally, for the benefit of SAUNDERS) I'll take you to Joseph and Kitty.

LADY K. If ye hae business, Doctor, juist gae straucht aheid. I'll fin my ain wey to the paurlor, and Joseph can look efter me there.

SKINNER. Very well, my lady, if you will.

LADY K. Guidbye, the nou.

SKINNER. Goodbye.

(She leaves, and he turns into the room)

SAUNDERS. I fand Tam Forrest for ye, Doctor, but he
was sittin in the Sheep's Heid greitin fou, and I thocht
it wyce juist to tell him to mak his wey here ance he
was sober eneuch to walk straucht and no disgrace ye.

SKINNER. How fortunate. The more I live the more I see
the hand of God in all that happens. Go back to the
Sheep's Head, Saunders, and tell Tom Forrest that he
must on no account come near me. If remorse has
driven him to drink he will soon be shouting his sins
from the house-tops, and those of us who exercised
compassion towards him may be implicated in his
guilt.

SAUNDERS. But whar aboot the cause o yer daith, Doctor?

SKINNER. I am not going to die after all, Saunders. The
Lord has seen fit to save me to carry on His work.

SAUNDERS. To save ye?

SKINNER. Sir Colin Kilgallon has passed away after
another stroke. There will be no divorce case.

SAUNDERS. Yes. There will be no need to carry out the
plan we discussed, and I hope you will obliterate all
memory of it from your mind. Forget what I said too,
Saunders, about the weakness of my flesh. You will
know that even the best of us are so sorely tried at
times that we fall by the wayside. Your house-keeper
used to unburden her soul to me, Saunders, when she
was more than usually distressed, and she spared me
no details.

(SAUNDERS gives an inarticulate grunt)

Yes. So you will be the soul of discretion. Nothing
must happen to impede our work. Allan Ramsay the
bookseller threatens to build a theatre in Carruber's
Close. We must stop him.

SAUNDERS. Ay, Doctor.

SKINNER. Hurry off to the Sheep's Head, then, Saunders, and make sure that Tom Forrest knows he must stay away.

SAUNDERS. Ay, Doctor.

SKINNER. Thank you.

(SKINNER conducts him to the door, and they leave.)

EPILOGUE

(The Saltmarket, Edinburgh.

As Prologue, except that the baggage carried by the caddies consists of coils of rope rather than cases of pictures.)

TOWN CRIER. Signor Emilio Bellini and his son Signor Guido, that hae performed on the ticht raips mony hazardous wonders in aa the capitals o Europe, will on Friday neist at three in the efternune, afore ony that care to assemble, walk a raip streitchit atween the hauf mune battery in the Castle, and a lum heid in Brodie's Loan on the sooth side o the Gressmercat, firin a pistol, baitin a drum, and performin a variety o ither antics on the wey. Collection. Collection. Collection.

(Street cries, music, etc., then the characters of the play enter for the last time to take their bow, MRS LUCY LINDSAY, perhaps, appearing from her sedan chair.)

OTHER C AND B PLAYSCRIPTS

* hardcover, + paperback

* All plays marked thus are represented for dramatic
presentation by C and B (Theatre) Limited,
18 Brewer Street, London W1R 4AS